The Origins of Public High Schools

The Origins of Public High Schools

A Reexamination of the
Beverly High School Controversy

Maris A. Vinovskis

The University of Wisconsin Press

Published 1985

The University of Wisconsin Press
114 North Murray Street
Madison, Wisconsin 53715

The University of Wisconsin Press, Ltd.
1 Gower Street
London WC1E 6HA, England

First printing

Printed in the United States of America

For LC CIP information see the colophon

ISBN 0-299-10400-1

To

Bernard Bailyn and Richard Buel,

valued teachers who provided

guidance, patience, and inspiration

Contents

Tables and Figures

ix

FIGURES

Acknowledgments

The debts incurred in researching and writing any monograph are difficult to discharge. At best, we usually thank only a small portion of the many individuals and institutions whose support and encouragement were essential throughout the project.

A modest but essential grant from the National Institute of Education (NIE) of the U.S. Department of Education (Grant No. G79–0107) provided support for the initial gathering and analysis of the data for this investigation. Lana Muraskin, the project director at NIE for this grant, played a very important administrative and intellectual role in the early stages of this analysis. Additional assistance was provided later by small grants from the Spencer Foundation through the Department of Education and from the American Institutions Program at the University of Michigan.

Most of the archival work was done at the Beverly City Hall, the Beverly Historical Society, and the Essex Institute in Salem. Numerous individuals assisted me at those institutions and I want to especially thank Daniel Hoisington, director of the Beverly Historical Society, and Irene Norton, reference librarian of the Essex Institute, for their hospitality, guidance, and patience. Supplementary primary and secondary materials for this project were kindly provided at several other institutions such as the Baker Library (Harvard University), Beverly Public Library, Hatcher Graduate Library (University of Michigan), Lynn Historical Society, Lynn Public Library, Newburyport Public Library, U.S. Library of Congress, and Widener Library (Harvard University).

In order to obtain the records of the various churches in Beverly it was necessary to go to many of those churches still in operation today. I am grateful to the ministers of those churches and especially to Robert W. Lovett and Ruth Norwell for their cooperation and assistance.

I would also like to thank the editors of the *Journal of Interdisciplinary History* for permission to reprint a revised version of my essay, "Quantification and the Analysis of American Antebellum Education," which appeared in the Spring 1983 issue. Since this essay was produced as part of the U.S.-U.S.S.R. exchange on quantitative studies in history, I would like to acknowledge the advice and assistance of my American and Soviet colleagues who commented on an earlier draft of that paper.

The quality of the manuscript was considerably enhanced by the comments and suggestions received from scholars who read earlier versions of this book. Among those who took time away from their own research to assist me are David Angus, Francis Blouin, Martin Burke, William Gienapp, Raymond Grew, John Jackson, Carl Kaestle, Robert Lovett, Terrence McDonald, Jeffrey Mirel, Gerald Moran, William Reese, and Mills Thornton. Needless to say, they are in no way responsible for any of the errors of fact or interpretation still present in this volume. I am also grateful to Michael Katz for sharing his ideas with me about this project at a very early stage. While we may disagree about our interpretation of events in mid-nineteenth century Beverly, I am deeply indebted to him for his imaginative and pioneering work on this subject.

The staff at the University of Wisconsin Press has provided invaluable assistance in the preparation and publication of this book. I am especially grateful to Gordon Lester-Massman for his enthusiasm and support and to Jan Levine Thal for her excellent copyediting of the manuscript.

My largest debt, and one which I will have the most difficulty in discharging, is to my family without whose support, encouragement, and sacrifices this book would never have been written. Our son Andy cheerfully accepted the decision to shift our "vacations" from Ocean City, New Jersey, to the North Shore of Massachusetts so that I could work more effectively on this project. And my wife Mary provided assistance not only in programming the data, but also in patiently, and usually with good humor, extensively editing and rewriting the entire manuscript. Indeed, my only regret is that she did not agree to be a coauthor since the amount and quality of work she has put into this manuscript certainly entitle her to that designation.

The Origins of Public High Schools

Introduction

DURING the past fifteen years, the field of educational history has experienced two important intellectual upheavals: one prompted by the questioning by a group of revisionist scholars of the more traditional and positive interpretations of the origins and functioning of public schools and the other by the increasing use of quantitative data and social science analysis. These two developments have produced contrasting responses among educational historians. While the revisionist interpretations of American education have provoked considerable controversy and even indignation among some in the profession, the introduction and use of social science analysis has been generally welcomed and accepted by almost everyone in this field.[1]

The term "revisionist" has been applied to a group of scholars which includes Michael Katz, Alexander Field, Samuel Bowles, Herbert Gintis, and others who generally argue that educational reforms in antebellum America were imposed upon an unwilling working class by capitalists who saw in public education a means of molding and controlling future workers in order to minimize class tensions resulting from the industrialization of the American economy in the antebellum period. While these scholars by no means agree on all aspects of antebellum education, they do share a basic skepticism about the so-called humanitarian origins of common school reforms and their benefits for the workers.[2] The revisionists have had a major impact upon the field of educational history not only substantively, but also methodologically, as they are among the pioneers in applying social science analysis to historical problems. Interestingly, while most radical or left-oriented historians in other fields have tended to shun quantitative analysis, these revisionists in educational history have embraced it.

The revisionists have been strongly challenged in the past five years—especially by Diane Ravitch who has questioned not only their methodology and findings, but also their motivation.[3] This has led to angry and vociferous rebuttals from the revisionists and the entire field of educational history has been drawn into an ideological debate over the origins and functioning of public education in America.[4] Unfortunately, in this process the important methodological and substantive issues often have been glossed over or lost entirely in the more elusive and often counterproductive arguments over the motivations of the scholars involved.

My own interest in the history of education initially grew out of efforts to ascertain trends in nineteenth-century schooling which would help explain the declines in fertility during that period and also out of my interest in the economic productivity of antebellum education.[5] The questions raised by these studies as well as those generated by the discovery of strong rural-urban difference in antebellum education led to further work, with Carl Kaestle, on education in Massachusetts.[6]

Since most of the investigations of antebellum public schooling focus on the reform efforts of Horace Mann during his tenure as the first secretary of the Massachusetts Board of Education, our work on antebellum Massachusetts education led us to a reconsideration of the politics of educational reform and to the assessment of studies by revisionists which challenged the earlier accounts of Horace Mann's work. While drawing heavily upon the revisionist investigations for both methodological and substantive assistance, it appeared to us that the revisionists had overemphasized the role of the capitalists, especially the manufacturers, in the expansion and reform of antebellum Massachusetts education and had neglected the importance of other factors such as partisan politics or the role of the clergy.[7]

In analyzing the development of antebellum education, it appears that the nature and quality of the arguments set forth to identify and explain the critical issues depend in large part upon the type of materials being considered. It is difficult to resolve disputes involving literary evidence when a scholar brings to the debate evidence that is influenced in part by his or her own biases which make it hard to prove or disprove any hypothesis. The debate often becomes a matter of marshalling quotations from the primary sources into opposing ranks. It is easier to settle differences, when those disagreements are amenable to resolution, by testing or retesting quantifiable data. Each disputant is forced to specify exactly what he or she is analyzing and to produce the statistical results which either confirm or disprove the hypothesis. This is not to imply, however, that the only or even the most important questions are those that are quantitative. Indeed, since so much of the current debate is over the intentions of the reformers, it is essential that work continue on these methodologically more difficult topics as well.[8] Nevertheless, it seems advantageous to focus, whenever possible, on areas of difference between the revisionists and nonrevisionists that can be analyzed using social science techniques.

In these debates over the origins and nature of antebellum education, one issue that frequently divides scholars and seems especially suited for further scientific inquiry is the controversy that arose over the establishment of a public high school in Beverly, Massachusetts, in the decades prior to the Civil War. Facing a likely indictment by the state for failing to maintain a public high school, the Beverly town clerk recorded the names of all of those who voted for or against establishing a public high school in the town. As far as we know, this is the only set of individual-level voting data on the preferences of ordinary nineteenth-century citizens regarding public high schools. Michael Katz used these data to demonstrate empirically the revisionist interpretation of the past. Using the list of voters who supported or opposed Beverly High School in 1860 and combining it with individual-level socioeconomic and demographic data from the federal census and local tax lists, Katz's analysis revealed that educational reforms were imposed upon the workers in that community by the wealthier citizens. Only the outbreak of the shoe strike in Massachusetts emboldened the workers to rebel against the capitalists and their high school and to resoundingly defeat authorization of the high school at the town meeting on March 14, 1860.[9]

At the time, the abolition of Beverly High School was a local matter and few beyond Beverly's borders were even aware of the school's demise. Today, however, the unique data produced by that controversy have placed the issue of Beverly High School at center stage in the debate between the revisionists and their critics. In addition, Katz's analysis of the Beverly High School controversy is regarded by most scholars as an innovative example of the employment of and a persuasive illustration of the usefulness of social science techniques in historical analysis. Indeed, even nonrevisionists often praise this work as "a brilliant study of nineteenth-century educational reform."[10] Similarly, a recent reassessment of antebellum educational development which differs significantly in its findings from those of Katz nevertheless acknowledges that this earlier work is "in many respects still the best" of the revisionist studies.[11] Even Ravitch, one of Katz's severest critics, concedes that this volume "has been one of the most significant books in its field during the past decade."[12]

Among revisionists, Katz's analysis of the Beverly High School crisis has not been questioned. His findings form the cornerstone of each of many other revisionist interpretations of this period and are essential to their arguments because Katz's analysis is one of the few empirical investigations that appears to lend strong support to the contention that capitalists imposed educational reforms upon a working class that was uninterested in and perhaps even hostile toward education.[13]

Initially some reviewers expressed reservations about the evidence and interpretations provided by Katz's analysis of the Beverly High School incident, but now most historians accept his analysis and incorporate the results of this important case study into an overall picture of antebellum education.[14] Recently, however, there has been a sharp attack upon the revisionists in general and Katz's study of the Beverly High School episode in particular. In a scathing but quite thoughtful consideration of Katz's analysis of the vote on the Beverly High School, Ravitz challenged not only his analysis, but the validity of those other revisionist interpretations of America's educational past which rely upon his case study.[15] In an angry reply, Katz dismissed Ravitch's challenges as groundless and reaffirmed his earlier interpretation of that event in Beverly.[16]

My initial examination of Katz's analysis of the controversy over the establishment of Beverly High School led me to question the strong conclusions that he was willing to draw from this analysis based as they were on limited statistical techniques. Rather than employ some form of multivariate analysis, Katz relied upon cross-tabulation of his data, making it virtually impossible for him to rate the relative importance of the various characteristics of the voters that might have determined whether they supported the high school.[17] My reservations about his statistical analysis encouraged me to consider reanalyzing these data, and the increasingly frequent citation of this particular study as evidence against the more complex interpretation of antebellum educational politics put forth by Kaestle and myself made the reconsideration of this study even more imperative.[18] Thus, a thorough reanalysis of the Beverly High School controversy from a broader perspective, one which would use more sophisticated statistical techniques, seemed to be the logical next step of the investigation into the question of the origins and functioning of antebellum public education.[19]

If the debate over the revisionist view of antebellum education stimulated me to consider undertaking this reanalysis of the Beverly High School controversy, the need for more detailed local studies of educational development reinforced in me the desire to execute this study. Recent statistical analyses of educational development at the state level have usually used aggregate town-level data.[20] While these studies are helpful in understanding the nature of schooling in states such as the Common-wealth, they are limited by the authors assuming that cities and towns throughout Massachusetts are reasonably homogeneous units. As this study of Beverly will demonstrate, there were measurable socioeconomic and geographic differences within Beverly as well as variations in the amount and type of schooling available to students. These factors had a significant impact on the development of education and their inclusion in the analysis engenders some very different results.[21]

When Katz discussed the origins and demise of Beverly High School, he devoted little attention to the overall development of public education in that community.[22] As a result, one does not know whether the workers opposed the establishment of Beverly High School in particular or op-posed public education in general. A more detailed analysis of education in Beverly would not only provide insights into the functioning of ante-bellum education, but might shed light on the crisis over the high school.

Another factor prompting this study is the need for a more thorough analysis of the origins of public high schools in America. Most of the re-cent investigations of antebellum education have focused on common schools and there is little work on the rise of public high schools.[23] The only major recent study of antebellum high schools is the one by Katz, which is now the center of considerable controversy.[24] Therefore, an analysis of the establishment and abolition of the Beverly High School in the late 1850s should provide additional information about antebellum public high schools and should stimulate further study of this relatively neglected but very important area in the history of American educa-tion.[25]

In an attempt to place the debate over the Beverly High School contro-versy in a broader context, chapter one will evaluate recent efforts to use quantification in the analysis of antebellum education. This overview will not only review recent examples of the application of social science methodology to the study of educational developments in the past, but will also clarify the strengths and weaknesses of this approach in the study of history. Since Katz's investigation of Beverly High School was a pioneering social science effort, it will be easier to acknowledge its im-portant place in the field as well as to evaluate its current applicability in light of more recent conceptual and methodological improvements in this area.

After the introduction to the use of quantification and the analysis of antebellum education, the focus will shift to the study of the Beverly High School controversy. Chapter two will analyze overall educational developments in Beverly not only to place the public high school debates in context, but also to ascertain the attitudes and actions of Beverly citizens toward education in general. In the next chapter, the origins of the Beverly High School will be traced not only within that community, but also as part of the state-wide efforts to promote and establish public high schools in the Commonwealth in the four decades prior to the Civil War. Chapter four will focus on the vote on the Beverly High School in 1860 and provide the most direct retest of Katz's statistical analysis. Finally, the volume will conclude with a recapitulation of the most important findings from this case study and their implications for the future study of antebellum education and the use of social science analysis.

Since so much of this work builds upon the pioneering efforts of Katz, it is important that the reader consult Katz's original work on this topic.[26] As part of an ongoing quest for understanding the origins and functioning of public education in antebellum America, it is only logical and fair that these two studies be read in conjunction with each other so that readers may decide for themselves what happened in Beverly on March 14, 1860, why it occurred, and what it tells us about nineteenth-century educational expansion and reform.

1 / Quantification and Analysis of
American Antebellum Education

DURING most of the twentieth century, analysis of educational history in the United States was a relatively undeveloped and narrowly focused field. Many of the practitioners were located in schools of education and produced mainly laudatory narratives of the rise of mass education or self-congratulatory histories of individual institutions. Some high-quality monographs on American educational development were produced, but these studies were neither typical products of the field as a whole nor particularly influential among historians.

In the past fifteen years, however, there has been a dramatic increase in the quantity and quality of work in educational history. Education in the past is now being analyzed from the broad perspective of the transmission of culture, including and expanding on the narrowly focused perspective of the development of public schools used in earlier studies. Furthermore, a new generation of historians has brought to the study of educational history many of the concepts and techniques of the "new" social and economic histories. The analysis of quantitative educational data has become a routine part of work in the field and has led to a series of stimulating monographs on educational developments in the past. No longer a minor subspeciality, educational history has become a major component in "new" social and economic histories of the United States.

This transition has not always been smooth and uneventful. Some recent studies in American educational history have provoked considerable controversy. The strong and sometimes acrimonious disagreements within the field today are not, however, over the desirability of using social science techniques, but rather concern the ideological orientations of the scholars and the political implications of their work. Once introduced into educational history, social science methodology was accepted quickly and quietly by most of the leading scholars in the field, while in other areas of history the applicability of these methods continues to divide the profession. The rapid acceptance of these newer methods has not been without flaws, however receptive the practitioners have been to this general approach. Sometimes these new tools of analysis have been adopted before conceptual and methodological difficulties about the applicability of particular social science techniques were adequately explored. This chapter will provide an introduction to many of the recent developments, illustrating some of the strengths and weaknesses of this new approach without trying to provide a synthesis or a resolution of all the issues raised.[1]

While it might be desirable to survey the entire field of American educational history, this chapter will focus on recent research in the area of antebellum education. The analysis of educational developments in antebellum America has become a focal point in many of the current controversies in this field. Furthermore, educational studies of the antebellum period have generally been among the most sophisticated and imaginative from a social science perspective so that an examination of them provides a reasonable introduction to the use of quantitative data for understanding American educational development. Confining our attention to the antebellum period will necessitate the omission of many interesting studies from this review, but it is hoped that by focusing on three major areas of research—the development of mass education, the determinants of school attendance, and the politics of antebellum school reform—it will be possible to provide a useful context in which to place the debate over the establishment and abolition of the Beverly High School.

THE DEVELOPMENT OF MASS EDUCATION

Much of the effort in the analysis of antebellum education has been to identify the development of mass education, to locate it in the two decades before the Civil War, and to explain it as a reaction to the social tensions produced by the industrialization of American society. Unfortunately, lumping all three of these themes together erroneously assumes that these occurred concurrently. Bowles and Gintis, for example, confidently assert that "educational reform and expansion" were the direct result of changes in the economy during this period:

> There can be little doubt that educational reform and expansion in
> the nineteenth century was associated with the growing ascendancy

of the capitalist mode of production. Particularly striking is the recurring pattern of capital accumulation in the dynamic advanced sectors of the economy, the resulting integration of new workers into the wage-labor system, the expansion of the proletariat and the reserve army, social unrest and the emergence of political protest movements, and the development of movements for educational expansion and reform. We also find a recurring pattern of political and financial support for educational change. While the impetus for educational reform sometimes came from disgruntled farmers or workers, the leadership of the movements—which succeeded in stamping its unmistakable imprint on the form and direction of educational innovation—was without exception in the hands of a coalition of professionals and capitalists from the leading sectors of the economy.[2]

These recent attempts to explain the rise of mass education in nineteenth-century America are seriously weakened by both conceptual and statistical difficulties. For instance, there is a tendency to use the terms educational "expansion" and "reform" interchangeably—as if these two different aspects of educational development were part of the same effort. Educational expansion is not necessarily the same as educational reform either chronologically or conceptually. Furthermore, few of the analyses of educational expansion have specified whether they wish to focus on the increasing literacy of the American population, the expansion of formal schooling, or the shift from private to public education. These distinctions are important because these aspects of educational development did not occur simultaneously and were often the result of different factors.

Almost all of the detailed work linking industrial development to the rise of mass education has used events in Massachusetts to illustrate local and national trends. Typically, the appointment of Horace Mann as the secretary of the Massachusetts Board of Education is used to date both educational expansion and reform in that state as well as in the country as a whole because his tenure in office coincided with the industrialization of the Commonwealth:

> Rapid growth in attendance paralleled these dramatic changes in the legal, financial and social structure of U.S. education. Twenty years before the Civil War, just under 38 percent of white children aged five-nineteen were attending schools. By 1860, the figure had risen to 59 percent. Thus Mann's ascendancy to the newly created Massachusetts State Board of Education in 1837, marked a major turning point in U. S. social history. For a period of comparable

importance, we must await the evolution of corporate capitalist production and the closely associated Progressive Education movement around the turn of the present century.[3]

Although one might legitimately link the advent of many educational reforms with the appointment of Mann as secretary of the Massachusetts Board of Education, at least for that state, one cannot equally identify the onset of educational expansion with him. Well before he became involved in educational reform, the people of Massachusetts were going to school in large numbers and were highly literate. As Kenneth Lockridge has argued, by the end of the eighteenth century, male literacy in New England was nearly universal and nearly half of New England women were also literate. Furthermore, school enrollment rates in Massachusetts were already high by 1800—with a large proportion of those children in school attending publicly supported schools. As a result, efforts to link (through Horace Mann) the rise of public education in Massachusetts with industrialization in that state are simply incorrect chronologically. When confronting the hard issues of levels of literacy and of school enrollments, educational reformers like Mann were really trying to maintain the existing high levels in the face of mounting problems created by the socioeconomic changes in the state, as well as by the recent influx of Irish immigrants.[4]

If increases in literacy and school enrollment rates cannot be explained as a response to industrial development in Massachusetts, perhaps other educational changes such as the increases in the length of the public school year were related to industrialization. Alexander Field, one of the more statistically sophisticated analysts of antebellum educational history, examined, using multiple regression analysis, the socioeconomic determinants of the variations in the length of the public school year in 1855 among 329 Massachusetts communities. He argued that the length of the public school year to be found in any one town reflected the commitment of elites in that town to educational reform since, according to his analysis, the length of the school year represented the amount of education that was supplied rather than the amount demanded (which, he says, would have been reflected by school enrollment rates).[5]

His analysis seems to show that the length of the public school year in 1855 was strongly positively related to the percentage of Irish people in the population, the family-per-dwelling ratio, and an index of merchants in the labor force. Accepting the length of the public school year as a measure of community interest in education, Field concluded that "the relationship between the length of school session on the one hand, and density, the share of Irish, and the share of merchants, on the other hand, revealed the intent of elite groups to use the schools as universal agencies of socialization.''[6]

Although Field has done a competent job of running his cross-sectional regressions for 1855, he has not made a convincing case for the length of the public school year as a reliable index of commitment to educational reform in the antebellum period—particularly among merchants and manufacturers. In part, his analysis is flawed because he assumed that cross-sectional relationships in this situation reflected longitudinal changes. His study implicitly assumed that the major improvements in the length of the public school year occurred in the larger and more commercialized areas of the state as local elites in those communities expanded public education to socialize the newly arriving Irish immigrants, as well as the native-born workers who were uprooted by industrial and commercial developments within the state. Although Field's cross-sectional regression analysis lends credence to such an interpretation, there are strong reasons to suspect that the relationship would not remain if he were to use longitudinal data. Assembling and organizing data on the length of the public school year by the size of the community in 1826, 1840, 1860, and 1875, suggests that Field may have missed some of the important dynamics of this process (see table 1.1).

The length of the public school year in Massachusetts did increase from 146 days in 1840 to 177 days in 1875, but the location of those increases within particular categories of Massachusetts towns is quite different from that suggested by Field's analysis. Field would have us believe that the increases in the public school year occurred in the more urban and industrial communities. As table 1.1 suggests, in reality the causes of the overall lengthening of the public school year may have been just the opposite of what Field proposed. Although the length of the

Table 1.1. Average Length (in days) of Massachusetts Public School Sessions, by Town Size, 1826, 1840, 1860, 1875

Town Size	1826	1840	1860	1875
0–1,249	127	136	137	154
1,250–2,499	143	138	147	176
2,500–4,999	172	160	172	188
5,000–9,999	204	197	200	205
10,000 and up	n.a.	246	231	215
Boston	n.a.	264	229	202
All towns	n.a.	146	159	177

Source: Carl F. Kaestle and Maris A. Vinovskis, *Education and Social Change in Nineteenth-Century Massachusetts* (Cambridge, England, 1980), pp. 25, 261.

public school year in small, rural communities grew substantially, it stayed the same or even declined in the larger urban areas such as Boston. Any definitive explanation of the relationship between the length of the public school year and the extent of urban or industrial development of the town must await a more sophisticated regression analysis over time, but these preliminary results (in table 1.1) are sufficiently clear and consistent to suggest that Field as well as many other scholars have tried to explain educational changes by focusing only on developments in urban areas. They have neglected, almost entirely, the crisis of rural education in nineteenth-century America where enrollment rates were high but financial resources to maintain public schools were very low compared to those in urban areas. While the expansion and improvement in urban education focused more on efforts to increase school enrollment rates and regularity of attendance, rural areas tried to increase the amount of education that they provided by lengthening the public school year in their districts. By relying exclusively on his cross-sectional analysis, Field missed this important distinction and neglected to differentiate among the types of problems facing different Massachusetts communities in their efforts to improve the quantity and quality of education for their children.[7]

The linkage of the rise of mass public education with urbanization and industrialization is further weakened when we consider educational developments outside Massachusetts. Analyses by scholars such as

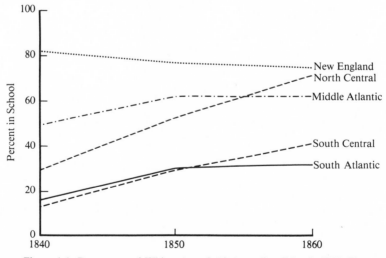

Figure 1.1. Percentage of Whites Ages 0–19 Attending School, 1840–60

Bowles and Gintis, for example, which focus almost entirely on Massachusetts where rapid industrialization was occurring in the decades before the Civil War, do not satisfactorily account for the tremendous growth of public schooling in the highly agricultural areas of the rest of the nation. If we look at the percentage of whites ages five through nineteen attending school from 1840 to 1860, we find that the largest increases in the rate of school enrollment occurred in the south central and north central states (see figure 1.1). New England actually experienced a slight decline in the rate of school enrollment during the period of time which Bowles and Gintis associate with the rise of mass public education.[8]

Another perspective on the development of education in antebellum America is obtained by calculating the percentage of change in the total number of students enrolled in school from 1840 to 1860 (see figure 1.2). The increase in the number of students attending school in New England accounted for only 2.7 percent of the total growth in school attendance from 1840 to 1860, while the increase in the number of students in the north central states accounted for 55.7 percent of that overall change. As Fishlow demonstrated in 1966, the rise of mass education in antebellum America was due more to the expansion of school attendance in the rapidly growing agricultural states of the north central and south central regions than to changes in the older and industrializing areas of the Northeast.[9]

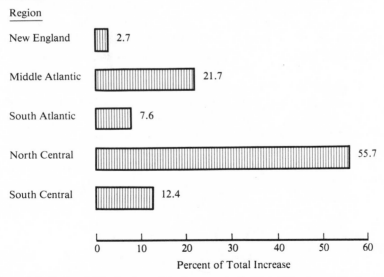

Figure 1.2. Regional Distribution of the Increase in the Total Number of Students Attending U.S. Schools, 1840–60

The emphasis placed on the rise of mass public education as a response to the economic and social unrest generated by industrial development in antebellum America ignores the fact that much of this educational expansion occurred in areas which were mainly agricultural. In general, most American historians writing during the late 1960s and 1970s have overemphasized the importance of the difficulties in urban or industrial areas in antebellum society by ignoring almost totally the problems associated with trying to "civilize" the rapidly growing West during this period.[10]

Any coherent explanation of the development of mass education will have to be based on a more complete understanding of the complex process of educational change in America. Instead of locating the origin of the rise of mass education temporally in the two decades before the Civil War and locating it geographically in Massachusetts, we need to trace the actual origins of that effort many decades earlier and include sufficient area to be able to account for the significant regional differences. First, New England Puritans laid the foundations of educational development in colonial times by insisting on literacy as an indispensable component of their religious functioning. Yet, it will also be necessary to explain the relative lack of development of mass education in the colonial South which led to distinct north-south differences in schooling and literacy not only in the colonial period but also in the nineteenth century.

Second, with the establishment of the new republic, the power of the electorate expanded considerably and necessitated educated citizens. Political leaders quickly recognized and acknowledged the importance of schooling and this political interest led to the push for education in the older, settled areas as well as to the expansion of education into the new territories and states of the West. Finally, the problems of creating and maintaining a system of mass public education will have to be differentiated by the needs and resources of the areas involved. The differences between rural and urban areas in the types of educational problems that they faced as well as in their relative economic abilities should be considered. In this larger synthesis, the current emphasis on the role of the manufacturers in the creation and maintenance of mass public education will become just one part of the whole explanation of the development of public education in the United States.

DETERMINANTS OF SCHOOL ATTENDANCE

The study of the patterns and determinants of school attendance has produced some of the most interesting and sophisticated analyses of antebellum education. Using individual-level data from the manuscript censuses, historians have analyzed the socioeconomic variations in the pattern of school attendance. While most analyses of the rise of mass education are more theoretical and speculative than empirical, the reverse tends to characterize the studies of individual-level school attendance.

Much of the interest in analyzing patterns of school attendance stems from the work of Thernstrom in the mid-1960s. Thernstrom analyzed the social mobility of laborers in Newburyport, Massachusetts, from 1850 to 1880 using individual-level data from the federal manuscript censuses. He found that social mobility for laborers was more limited than suggested by nineteenth-century observers, even though a substantial portion of the Newburyport laborers who remained in that community were able to accumulate significant amounts of property. Thernstrom found that the very process of acquiring property was detrimental to the educational prospects for the laborers' children and thus explained, in part, their limited social mobility. Furthermore, Thernstrom stressed the importance of ethnic and religious rather than class differences among laborers in explaining school attendance:

> That Irish working class families were especially successful in accumulating property but especially unsuccessful in climbing out of the low-status manual occupations was hardly a coincidence. The immigrant laborer received wages no higher than those of the Yankee workman, but he had a greater determination to save and to own. Perhaps the land hunger displayed by the Irish laborers of Newburyport was a manifestation of older peasant values. In any case, it was a hunger which could be satisfied to a remarkable extent even by the lowliest laborer—but only at a price. The price was not only ruthless economy; equally necessary was the employment of every able-bodied member of the family at the earliest possible age. The cotton mill or the shoe factory was not to provide the teenagers of the second generation with the education made increasingly necessary by a rapidly industrializing economy, as the exceptionally low mobility of Irish youths into nonmanual occupations so plainly reveals.[11]

Thernstrom's analysis of school attendance was expanded and improved by Katz in his study of mid-nineteenth-century Hamilton, Ontario. While agreeing with Thernstrom that education may have been an important factor in individual social mobility, Katz stressed that the marginal advantages of extended education which in theory would benefit all classes of students in practice were reserved for the children of the most privileged families. "Thus, the rise in school attendance did not destroy—or even seriously alter—the connection between education and class. In this way education has helped to sustain and reproduce the class relations of a capitalist society.''[12]

Katz also disagreed with Thernstrom's conclusion about the importance of ethnicity or religion in determining the likelihood of children attending school. Instead, he argued that these ethnic and/or religious factors were merely stand-ins for the true differentiator—class:

> With a couple of exceptions, the ethnic differences in the relationship between the age of leaving school and home, or undertaking work and marriage, appear to have resulted from class distinctions. It was the ethnic group most clearly associated with lower-class standing, the Irish Catholics, that differed most sharply from the others. And those differences by and large had been shaped by class: lower rates of school attendance, higher rates of adolescent employment, and consequently earlier ages of leaving home.[13]

The debate over the relative importance of ethnicity and religion or occupational class in determining patterns of school attendance has been the major area of disagreement among historians. The effects of other variables such as age or sex on school enrollment provoked much less concern and debate.

Methodological differences, however, soon became another major source of disagreement among analysts of patterns of school attendance based on individual-level data. One of the difficulties of analyzing school enrollment figures using aggregate data was the tendency to lump children of all ages together. Even when individual-level data were available, it was a common practice to combine figures for children attending school who were ages five to fifteen or five to sixteen. Although efforts were sometimes made to distinguish between data for younger and older children, few of these early analyses controlled for age effectively, nor did they differentiate the importance of education for the child's educational development by his or her age.[14]

Recently, historians of education have paid much more attention to the age of the child attending school. The pattern of nineteenth-century school attendance is now frequently subdivided into three broad categories—entry into school (usually ages four to eight), a period of high, even near universal, attendance (usually ages nine to twelve), and the time of school leaving (usually ages thirteen to nineteen). These three divisions, used initially by Kaestle and Vinovskis to analyze patterns of school attendance in eight Essex County (Massachusetts) communities in 1860 and 1880, are useful since mid-nineteenth-century Americans differentiated the value of education roughly along these lines.[15]

The attitudes of nineteenth-century Americans toward the importance of education for those three age groups were not always the same. The desirability of early childhood education was by turns in and out of favor. During the first third of the nineteenth century there was considerable emphasis on the desirability of sending very young children (ages two to four) to infant schools. As late as 1840, almost 40 percent of three-year-olds in Massachusetts were in school. But in the second third of the nineteenth century there was a strong reaction among educators, doctors, and eventually parents against sending young children to school before the ages of five, six, or even seven for fear that their young minds would be permanently damaged by early intellectual training. As a result, when young rural and lower-class children continued to be sent to school sooner than urban and middle-class children, this was interpreted as a problem rather than as an advantage for those young children in school. Hence, analyses of the rates of school attendance which do not differentiate between early entry and early school leaving and which do not take into account the attitudes of nineteenth-century Americans fail to see the importance of that education as contemporaries judged it.[16]

Even though early education (at ages three, four, or five) was not favored in the mid-nineteenth century, there was a general agreement that all white children roughly between the ages of nine and twelve should be attending school. The value of common school education for all white children was widely shared and efforts were made to provide enough public facilities throughout the United States in the decades before the Civil War to achieve this goal. Consequently, in areas such as Essex County where almost everyone between the ages of nine and twelve was in school, class or ethnic differences could not play a significant role in predicting patterns of school attendance.[17]

Since most studies of individual-level school attendance have been done as part of larger analyses of urban society and have employed the research designs commonly used in urban history, they suffer from some of the same deficiencies that characterize much of urban history today. A fundamental weakness of much of urban history is the reliance on single community research for multi-community or regional conclusions. This almost exclusive focus on single urban communities has been unfortunate in at least two respects. First, little effort has been made to design research projects that include different types of urban and industrial developments for comparative purposes. Second, the reliance on urban areas has made it impossible to separate the effects of urban development from more general changes within that society. In other words, by not having any rural areas for comparison in their analyses, researchers cannot be certain whether the changes experienced by any group over time within a city are the result of the impact of urbanization on their lives or the consequence of more general developments within that society as a whole. Thus, we cannot be certain whether the increases in rates of school attendance by older children in Hamilton from 1851 to 1871 are the result of increased interest in education as the city became industrialized or whether they merely reflect the general growing interest in education throughout Canadian society during those years.[18]

There are ways to improve upon the single community focus. One might study several different communities which include both rural and urban areas. One such example is the study by Kaestle and myself of eight Essex County communities in 1860 and 1880 to analyze variations in the pattern of school attendance by taking into consideration the interaction between community structure and family life in one small area. By restricting the analysis to eight communities within one county, we minimized any regional differences in our analysis. We do not claim that this particular county is in any way typical or representative of the country as a whole, but only that the diversity of activities within it permits interesting and useful analyses at both the community and household levels.[19]

The communities selected within Essex County provided a variety of experiences and opportunities for their inhabitants. We chose three large, urban areas each having different types of economic activity—Lawrence, Lynn, and Salem. Lawrence was a new city developed around the textile industry; Lynn was an old city dominated by the shoe industry; and Salem was an old commercial center that became heavily industrialized only after the Civil War. In addition, we selected five rural areas—Boxford, Hamilton, Lynnfield, Topsfield, and Wenham. Although all of these communities had small populations, they varied in their economic activities. Some, like Boxford, were almost totally agricultural, whereas others, like Lynnfield, had a sizable portion of their population already engaged in the shoe industry.

In our analysis of school leaving, we discovered that even after controlling for the effects of other variables, youths went to school at greater rates in the rural areas of Essex County. Comparing 1860 and 1880 figures, we note a rough and imperfect convergence of rural and urban educational experiences. Our analysis of these eight Essex County towns, however, still shows substantial differences in enrollment patterns in 1880. Although there were some differences in rates of school attendance among the three urban communities in both 1860 and 1880, they were less pronounced than one might have expected given the diversity of the economic activities of the three cities.[20]

Another methodological issue separating, at least initially, some of the analysts of school attendance was a debate over the use of statistical procedures such as cross-tabulation and multiple regression analysis. One reason that Thernstrom and Katz have had such difficulty in agreeing on the relative importance of ethnicity or occupation in determining school attendance may be that they relied on simple cross-tabulation of their data which did not allow them to control effectively for the influence of other variables. When Katz was criticized by Denton and George for not using multivariate analysis, Katz not only questioned the manner in which Denton and George presented their own multiple regressions, but also suggested that cross-tabulation was a better statistical procedure than multivariate analysis. This rather lively debate nicely illustrates some of the growing pains of educational history since few statisticians today would try to defend the superiority of cross-tabulating data if one could legitimately and carefully employ some form of multivariate analysis. Indeed, Katz has gone on to use multivariate analyses effectively in his more recent studies of the determinants of school attendance.[21]

In order to test the relative importance of occupational class and ethnicity in determining school attendance of older children, Kaestle and I included these variables in our multiple classification analysis of eight Essex County communities. In both 1860 and 1880, the ethnicity of the child was a slightly better predictor of his or her school attendance than the occupation of the parent. Since multiple classification analysis assumes the relative independence of the predictor variables, we reran the MCA after combining the variables of ethnicity and occupation into a new variable. The results confirmed that even after controlling for the effects of occupational differences (as well as for other variables), ethnicity continued to exert a major influence on patterns of school attendance. Foreign-born children of white-collar and skilled workers attended school at substantially lower rates than the native-born children of even semi-skilled and unskilled parents. Although we found that the occupation of the parents was an important predictor of school attendance of older children, it did not eliminate the negative impact of being foreign born on the likelihood of attending school. It is interesting that when Katz and Davey reran their data on school attendance for Hamilton using multiple classification analysis, the ethnicity of the child continued to be an important predictor, even after controlling for the effects of the economic variables.[22]

Although educational historians gradually seem to be reaching more of a consensus on the use of statistics and on the importance of both class and ethnicity in predicting school attendance, several issues still remain to be explored. One particularly intriguing problem in most of these studies concerns using the occupation of the head of the household as the index of the household's well-being without taking into consideration the number of other wage earners and dependents in that family. Recently several scholars have tried to develop a broader approach to this issue. Although the occupation of the parent is a useful and important indicator of the economic situation of the family, it is not the only economic datum we would like to use. Ideally, we would measure the actual consumption needs of the family, as several contemporary studies have done. Unfortunately, the appropriate data were not collected in the nineteenth-century censuses. We can go beyond using just the occupation of the head of the household, however, by taking into consideration the number of individuals in the family who are employed as well as the number of consumers within the family.

Since the earning and consuming ability of individuals varies by age and by sex, we adjusted our data with a set of weights to take these factors into consideration. Our work/consumption index is obtained by dividing the number of working units in each family by the number of consuming units. Although this index does not fully capture the individual family variations in income and consumption needs, it does provide a rough measure of a whole family's economic situation and improves on information on the head of the household.[23]

This work/consumption index has been used in two different studies of the eight Essex County communities: one on school attendance and the second on women's labor force participation. In the labor force participation case the work/consumption index has proven to be useful. Surprisingly, however, the work/consumption index does not behave in the expected way in predicting whether older children stay in school. There are a variety of possible explanations for the failure of the work/consumption index to predict school attendance, ranging from the inadequacy of the index itself to the fact that leaving school did not necessarily mean that the child was forced to enter the labor force to help the family financially. In any case, we hope that other students of past family behavior will continue to develop indices like our work/consumption ratio that try to measure the economic situation of the entire family, rather than rely only on the occupation of the head of the household or on the size of the family.[24]

Finally, it is important to realize that the assumptions underlying some of the current work on school attendance are being inadvertently challenged by educational historians researching other topics. Both Thernstrom and Katz assumed in their analyses that education promoted social mobility and economic well-being. Thernstrom stressed the importance of changes in the actual amount of education received by individuals; Katz emphasized the significance of the relative amounts of education received by individuals as a way of perpetuating existing class distinctions.

Other historians, such as Field and Graff, have questioned the value of education in helping individuals to get ahead. Field stresses that nineteenth-century industrialization did not require additional skills, so that the rise of mass public education was not a response to industry demands for more trained workers, but an effort to socialize the labor force into accepting the changes and dislocations due to industrialization. Graff, analyzing three Canadian cities (including Hamilton), questions whether literate workers were any more successful than illiterate ones if we take into consideration their ethnic origins:

> Social thought and social ideals have, for the past two centuries, stressed the preemption of ascription by achievement as the basis of success and mobility, and the importance of education and literacy in overcoming disadvantages deriving from social origins. In the three cities, in 1861, however, ascription remained dominant. Only rarely was the achievement of literacy sufficient to counteract the depressing effects of inherited characteristics, of ethnicity, race, and sex. The process of stratification, with its basis in rigid social inequality, ordered the illiterates as it did those who were educated. Only at the level of skilled work and its rewards did literacy carry a meaningful influence. Literacy, overall, did not have an independent impact on the social structure; ethnicity primarily, mediated its role, while literacy largely reinforced that of ethnicity. . . . The possession of literacy alone rarely entailed occupational and economic gains; its benefits were very few in these areas, in sharp contrast to theory and assertions. Sex, ethnicity (especially Irish Catholicism), and race were far more important than literacy or education. Illiteracy of course was a depressing factor; the converse, however, did not hold true.[25]

If Graff's portrayal of the value of literacy, especially for the foreign born, is true, then Thernstrom's Irish laborers in Newburyport may have been wise to send their children to work rather than keep them in school. Before we conclude too hastily that middle- and upper-class parents who kept their children in school the longest were wasting their own resources and their children's time, however, we will need much more evidence on the rates of return to schooling in nineteenth-century America. Field and Graff may be correct that literacy was not of great assistance in the unskilled and semiskilled occupations, but this does not mean that it was not of considerable importance for skilled workers or professionals —whether as a credential-giving device or as an actual skill. For example, since about one-fifth of all antebellum Massachusetts women taught at some point in their lives, the acquisition of at least a common school education was of some benefit to at least a significant portion of the populace. Furthermore, although Graff has done the most extensive analysis of the advantages and disadvantages of literacy, it is not conclusive statistically since he did not control adequately for other factors and his sample size became very small when he divided his population into various subcategories.[26]

The estimation of the rates of return to education for the individual should become one of the major issues for educational historians and the results so far, although highly suggestive, are sufficiently limited or flawed that we must await improved studies before we can pass judgment on the value of education to individuals in nineteenth-century America.[27]

POLITICS OF ANTEBELLUM EDUCATIONAL REFORM

The issue in educational history which has attracted the most effort and generated the most controversy during the past fifteen years is the question of educational reform. Scholars such as Bowles, Field, Gintis, and Katz reject traditional explanations of antebellum educational reforms and postulate new ones which emphasize the role of manufacturers. Most of their work on this topic has centered on explaining Mann's activities and motivations as the secretary of the Massachusetts Board of Education.

Field contends that the manufacturers, often working through professionals, were the chief architects of the educational reforms commonly associated with Mann. To support this position, he assembled a variety of evidence, none of which is conclusive by itself, but all of which, he contends, supports his conclusions. For example, he investigated the occupations of the local school board members of the industrial town of Lowell, Massachusetts, as well as of the members of the Massachusetts Board of Education. But his evidence in both cases does little to support his interpretation of the pivotal role of manufacturers. Instead, professionals, particularly clergymen in the case of Lowell, seem to have been predominant on the board. Field dismisses this apparent contradiction by arguing that the manufacturers may have deliberately avoided such public posts in order to generate even greater support for the school reforms:

> The composition of the state board, and data from local school committees as well, indicate that manufacturers did participate directly in the politics of school administration. They struck a low

profile, however, perhaps because of the suffrage, and left much of the field open to professionals like Mann. Although such professionals might be aligned with manufacturing wealth, they were less publicly tied to property and could thus elicit wider support for the expansion of schooling.[28]

The cornerstone of Field's empirical demonstration of the crucial role of manufacturers in Massachusetts antebellum educational reforms therefore must rest almost entirely on his cross-sectional analysis of the determinants of the length of the public school year in 1855. Taking the length of the public school year as the index of support for educational commitment, Field stated in his dissertation that the results confirmed the role of manufacturing as the key element of educational reform: "Analysis of cross-section regression suggests that reform had the greatest success in the manufacturing, as opposed to urban-commercial or rural-agrarian areas, and particularly in manufacturing towns where the choice of technologies and work organizations involving the employment of large numbers of unskilled workers led to a large fraction of the labor force being Irish and living in very crowded conditions."[29]

When Field revised his analysis for publication, however, he responded to the recent developments in the field of educational history by including new variables such as the percentage of merchants in each community. As a result of these improvements, his findings changed and he no longer contends that manufacturing per se was an important predictor of the length of the public school year. Instead, the merchants are now portrayed as leaders of educational reform, whereas in his dissertation they were depicted more as acquiescing to the initiatives of the manufacturers working through local professionals. Thus, Field has arrived at a more balanced picture of educational reform that stresses the now seemingly equal efforts of "politically active, self-conscious groups of professionals, merchants and businessmen" rather than arguing for the pivotal role of manufacturers in this undertaking.[30]

The apparent evolution of Field's analysis of the politics of Massachusetts school reforms is not only interesting in itself, but is important for reassessing the arguments of others such as Bowles and Gintis. Since Bowles and Gintis did relatively little primary work on the politics of Massachusetts education, they relied heavily on the findings of Field's dissertation. Consequently, as Field revises his earlier interpretations of the importance of manufacturers in the process of educational reform, Bowles and Gintis will either have to revise their own position or produce new evidence to bolster it.[31]

One continual source of confusion in the analyses of antebellum reforms is that, although most scholars agree on the centrality of Mann in this effort, they often implicitly attribute all educational changes to his efforts and assume that the same coalition of individuals and groups backed all of the reforms. Yet the support for educational improvement in Massachusetts often varied from issue to issue. For example, the length of the public school year was of particular concern in the rural areas where the public schools were not kept open year round, but it was less of a problem for urban areas which already provided a long school year. Similarly, the support or opposition to the creation of public high schools should not be confused with popular endorsement of common schools. In addition, one wonders why the elites, supposedly mainly concerned about socializing workers, devoted so much of their energy and money to improving the quality of teacher training when they could have concentrated their efforts on getting children into school and keeping them there.[32]

It is time to differentiate among the various aspects of educational reform—especially when trying to explain the motivations of the diverse participants in this effort. Although distinguishing among the different aspects of educational reform will not lead so easily to a simple interpretation of educational reform, the interpretation will be much more accurate historically than many of the explanations that have been put forth so far.

The recent efforts to analyze the politics of educational reform have been surprisingly uninterested in Massachusetts politics. Rather than study the actual political battles over Mann's reforms, researchers have been content to measure support for his efforts indirectly by analyzing the composition of local school boards or by studying variations in the length of the school year.

In order to test the support for and opposition to Mann's reforms more directly, Kaestle and I investigated the effort to abolish the state Board of Education in the Massachusetts House of Representatives in March 1840 based on a roll-call analysis of the 519 members of that chamber. We encoded information on the personal characteristics of the members of the House as well as on their constituents and ran a multiple classification analysis of the representatives' support for or opposition to the Board of Education.

We discovered that there were substantive differences between the Whigs and Democrats, not only over the importance of common school education, but also over questions of state centralization of education and expenditures for teacher seminars. In fact, party affiliation was by far the single best predictor of one's vote. Representatives who were manufacturers were more apt to support the board than some other groups, yet nearly half of the Democratic manufacturers opposed the board. Furthermore, while representatives from areas with a high degree of manufacturing were supportive of the board, they were especially supportive when they were from areas which were also highly commercialized. Representatives from more industrialized but not highly commercialized communities were not particularly strong in their support of Mann and the board.[33]

Thus, an understanding of the support for or opposition to Mann's reform efforts must be intimately tied to understanding the larger political controversy within the Commonwealth over the proper role of the state in the development of common school education rather than just linked to the needs of a particular group such as manufacturers. It is interesting that there was almost no relationship between the length of the public school year in a representative's district and the way he voted on the issue of the Board of Education—reinforcing the point that different aspects of educational reform probably attracted varying sources of support from the ordinary citizenry as well as from the elites.[34]

As we have seen, many of the class-conflict interpretations of antebellum educational reform are coming under increasing scrutiny and revision. The debate over the nature of these reforms is intensifying rather than subsiding—probably an inevitable and not necessarily unwelcome development. Furthermore, due to the conceptual and methodological limitations inherent in the more indirect aggregate approaches to the study of educational reform, there is now even greater interest in the few local studies which provide a more detailed picture of the efforts to improve antebellum schooling. Particularly central to the class conflict interpretations of educational reform is Katz's now classic study of the abolition of the Beverly Public High School in 1860.[35]

Because they left so few written records, it is very difficult to document the reactions of workers to educational reforms. Katz ingeniously tried to solve this shortcoming by analyzing the pattern of voting when the citizens of Beverly voted to discontinue its two-year-old high school. His analysis was made possible by the unique circumstances in Beverly where the town clerk recorded how each of 392 citizens voted on the high school issue. Katz's study of this contest remains one of the most important investigations of local school politics and his conclusion that this episode revealed the class hostility of the workers against educational reforms has been accepted without question, not only by revisionists like Bowles, Gintis, and Field, but also by most other historians as well.[36] Since the analysis of the abolition of the Beverly Public High School remains so central to the interpretation of antebellum school reform and yet, as we shall see, may be flawed methodologically, it is important as a logical next step in the inquiry about the reactions of Americans to ante-bellum educational reforms to replicate and improve upon Katz's pioneering work. Therefore, the next three chapters will reanalyze in detail the origin and demise of the Beverly Public High School in the decades prior to the Civil War.

2 / Educational Developments
in Antebellum Beverly

ONE of the more typical and frustrating shortcomings in historical studies is the failure of scholars to define clearly certain key concepts or terms in their studies analyzing educational trends and reforms. Often the development of common schools is confused with other educational reforms or inappropriately linked to some individual educational reformer. Typically educational development and reforms in Massachusetts are equated with Horace Mann's becoming the first secretary of the Massachusetts Board of Education in 1837, or are identified with some particular aspect of educational reform such as the lengthening of the public school year, or are linked to the establishment of public high schools. None of these approaches by itself captures the complexity of the changes themselves or of the full range of factors influencing antebellum education.

In the work by Michael Katz, confusion arises because he sometimes seems to equate general antebellum educational reform with the rise of the public high school.[1] Such an equation would be appropriate only if the creation of public high schools was really what most people in antebellum Massachusetts meant when they spoke of educational developments and reforms. Certainly some of them did speak of the need for high schools, but most of the public concern about education, as well as the professional concern as voiced by educational reformers, was not directed at high schools but at the common schools—and most vocally in the 1830s and 1840s.[2] Therefore, even if the workers in Beverly had opposed unanimously the creation of the high school, it would not necessarily tell us anything about their attitudes and behavior toward popular education in general. In fact, it may be that many people favored the expansion of public education at the common school level, but opposed the apparently excessive cost of building and maintaining high schools for the few children in the community who used them. In this situation, would it be correct to say that the people opposed popular education simply because they opposed the high school?

In order to be able to paint a broader, more complete, and balanced picture of the attitudes of Beverly citizens toward education in the two decades before the Civil War, this chapter will attempt to sketch some of the general trends in educational developments in that community. To make this work comparative and meaningful, educational trends in Beverly will be compared and contrasted with those in the state as a whole (Massachusetts), the county in which it is located (Essex County), and another urban center just across the bay from Beverly (Salem). By analyzing the educational experiences of Beverly citizens from this larger perspective, perhaps we will be in a better position to understand the reasons for the creation and abolition of the Beverly Public High School.

TRENDS IN SCHOOL ATTENDANCE

Many historians have simply assumed that the percentage of persons ages 0-19 enrolled in public and private schools in Massachusetts rose dramatically from 1840 to 1860 as the result of Horace Mann's efforts.[3]

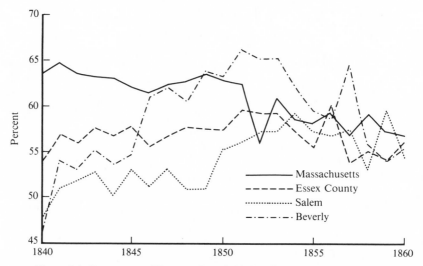

Figure 2.1. Percentage of Persons Ages 0–19 Enrolled in Schools, 1840–60

The actual trends, as first pointed out by Albert Fishlow, are quite different.[4] The percentage of children ages 0–19 declined from 63.7 percent in 1839–40 to 56.8 percent in 1859–60—an overall decline of 10.8 percent (see figure 2.1)

In Essex County, the percentage of persons ages 0–19 enrolled in all schools gradually rose from 50.7 percent in 1839–40 to 60.2 percent in 1855–56 and then declined to 56.2 percent in 1859–60. While the percentage of children under twenty enrolled in schools declined overall in Massachusetts, it remained relatively stable in Essex County.

In both Beverly and Salem, the percentage increased of children ages 0–19 who were enrolled. In Beverly, the percentage increased from 42.3 percent in 1839–40 to 55.4 percent in 1859–60—a rate of increase of 31.0 percent. In the larger seaport community of Salem across the bay, the percentage of persons ages 0–19 who were enrolled in all schools rose from 42.2 percent in 1839–40 to 54.4 percent in 1859–60—a slightly lower rate of increase than in Beverly. Thus, while the rates of school enroll-ment in Massachusetts as a whole declined and those in Essex County remained steady, both Beverly and Salem experienced sizable increases so that on the eve of the Civil War the rates at all four levels were almost identical.[5]

While the data on school enrollment may not be as accurate as we would like, a large part of the decrease in the rate of school enrollment in the state does appear to be a result of the decrease of four- and five-year-old children attending school. During the early nineteenth century, it was common for very young children to attend public or private schools since parents and educators thought that children should be taught to read as soon as possible. The infant school movement in America in the late 1820s and early 1830s reinforced the effort to send young children to school. But in the mid-1830s there was a strong reaction against sending such young children into the schools because doctors such as Amariah Brigham now argued that early intellectual activity would lead to insanity. Indeed, children under four were prohibited by the school committee from attending public schools in Beverly in the early 1840s.[6] Since very young children were more likely to be found attending school in 183⸝–40 in Massachusetts or Essex County than in either Beverly or Salem, the gradual elimination of these children from the schools reduced enrollment rates in the state and county more than in the latter two communities.

While the percentage of students rose in Salem and Beverly during these years, there was also a significant change in the proportion receiving their education from private schools—especially in the smaller and less-established ones which competed directly with the common schools for younger students. Many antebellum reformers put great emphasis on getting local communities to improve their common school facilities so that parents would send their children to public rather than to private schools. While the residents of Beverly welcomed the establishment of the privately incorporated Beverly Academy in 1833 intended for more advanced students, they sought to upgrade their public schools in order to minimize or eliminate the need for private elementary schools which catered to the younger students. The percentage of all students enrolled in private schools in Beverly dropped dramatically from 17.6 percent in 1839–40 to only 4.5 percent in 1859–60 (see figure 2.2). While the percentage of students in private schools in Salem was always high compared to the other communities, it also dropped from 22.5 percent of all enrolled students in 1839–40 to 18.7 percent in 1859–60. Although the decline in relative private school enrollments was less drastic in the state than in Beverly, Salem, or Essex County, it also decreased from 12.9 percent to 8.0 percent during this period.[7]

The reform efforts of Horace Mann and others were quite successful in encouraging families to send their children to public rather than to private schools—especially in communities such as Beverly where in 1840 nearly one-fifth of the children were in private schools but by the eve of the Civil War the overwhelming majority went to public schools. Shifting the control of such a large portion of education in the community from private hands to those of the town school committee and local districts was an important event that has gone largely unmentioned in most of the discussions of the debates over public education in Beverly.

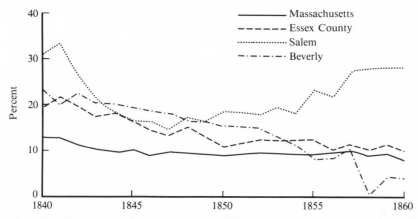

Figure 2.2. Percentage of Total Annual School Enrollment in Private Schools, 1840–60

The shift toward more public education in Beverly not only meant more public control, but also a shift in the payment for that education from the families of the private school children to those of the town as a whole. Interestingly, one does not find any evidence of protest or opposition in Beverly to this important change in education from private to public hands. If many of the residents of Beverly did not support a public high school in 1860, the majority of them either agreed or acquiesced in this shift from private to public education despite the increased tax burden.

Trends in total rates of annual school enrollment and in the proportion of students in private schools tell us nothing about the likelihood of students attending schools on a daily basis. Although enrollment rates give us an idea of how many children benefited from schooling at some point during the year, the rates of average daily attendance provide a more accurate measure of how much education children actually received each year.

In Beverly, the percentage of children under twenty who were attending school daily bulged upward from 28.4 percent in 1839–40 to 42.2 percent in 1850–51 and then subsided to 33.0 percent in 1859–60 (see figure 2.3). Overall, the average daily rate of school attendance in Beverly rose by a rate of 16.2 percent during these two decades—a somewhat slower rate of growth than the 31.0 percent rate of growth in the enrollment rate during the same period. Despite the improvements in Beverly, the average daily rate of school attendance still was lower there in 1859–60 than in Massachusetts, Essex County or Salem.

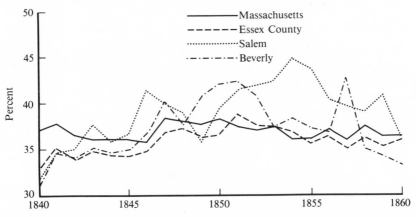

Figure 2.3. Average Daily Public and Private Attendance as a Percentage of All Children Ages 0–19, 1840–60

Children under twenty in Beverly in 1859-60, for example, attended school daily at a rate of 8.1 percent less than their counterparts in Salem. Although, as we saw earlier, the rates of school enrollment were almost identical in 1859-60, the daily attendance rates were not. An important difference between the two communities was that Salem pupils were considerably more regular in their attendance than Beverly students. It is not surprising to find that throughout the antebellum period, the Beverly School Committee stressed the importance of regular school attendance in its evaluations of the achievements of public school teachers. For example, in commenting upon the primary school in a section of Beverly called the Washington district, the committee observed:

> We were pleased to learn that there was during the term an average attendance of fifty scholars out of an entire number of fifty-seven. There is no better general criterion of the success of a school than the average attendance. When this has been as large as in the present instance, we may be pretty sure that the school has done its work well; and where the attendance is small, unless in the case of an epidemic, or an unusually severe season, or some other extraordinary obstacle, it may be taken as at the least extremely probable that there is something wrong about the school itself.[8]

Although the citizens of Beverly had made major improvements in education by increasing the rates of school enrollment and by shifting to public rather than private schools, they had not succeeded in convincing their students to attend school as regularly as did those in Massachusetts, Essex County, or Salem.

The average daily attendance rate of pupils gives us only a partial measure of the amount of education children received in antebellum Massachusetts. The other crucial piece of information we need is the average length of the school year. We do not have annual information on the length of the private school year (though we can make estimates), but we do have data on the average length of the public school year.

The average length of the public school year in Beverly increased from 195 days in 1839-40 to 203 days in 1858-59—an increase of 4.1 percent (see figure 2.4). In Salem, on the other hand, the average length of the public school year declined from 264 days in 1840-41 to 253 days in 1859-60—a decline of 4.2 percent.[9] Thus, though there was some convergence between the length of the public school year in Beverly and that in Salem, Salem continued to provide much more public education for its children than Beverly did. On the other hand, Beverly was providing as much public schooling as was available in the average community in Essex County and considerably more than in the state as a whole.

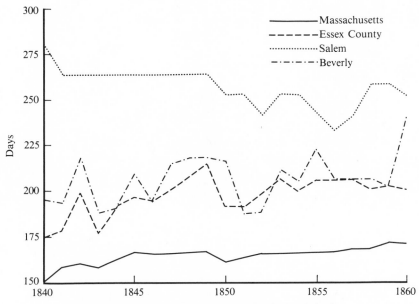

Figure 2.4. Length of Public School Sessions, 1840–60

Field uses the length of the public school year as an index of support for educational reforms in a community. By that criteria, Beverly displayed as much interest in education as the rest of the county, but much less than Salem did.[10] Since the length of the public school year in Salem was decreasing while it was increasing in Beverly, one might argue that there was a major reversal of emphasis on educational reform in these two communities. As discussed in the previous chapter, however, the length of the public school year probably is not a good enough index of overall interest in education to permit such speculation. Variations in the length of the public school year may in part simply reflect the differences in economic development. Salem, an urban area, provided year-round education while Beverly, still heavily agricultural in some areas, maintained a shorter school year in order to allow children to work in the fields.

Another view of school attendance can be obtained by combining the average daily attendance and the average length of the school year. The combination provides an estimate of the average number of days of public or private school attended annually per person under twenty years of age. In Beverly, the average number of days of school per person under twenty increased dramatically from 59.1 days in 1839–40 to 78.4 days in 1859–60—an overall increase of 32.7 percent (see figure 2.5). This is par-

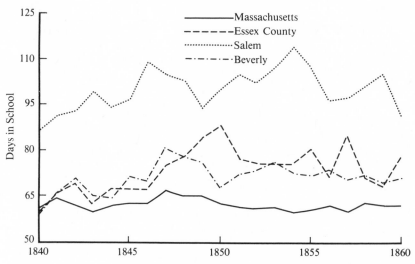

Figure 2.5. Average Number of Days of Public or Private School Attended per Person under 20 Years of Age, 1840–60

ticularly impressive compared to Salem which witnessed only a rise from 87.0 days in 1839–40 to 91.7 days in 1859–60—an increase of 5.4 percent. Thus, the children in Beverly were the recipients of increasing amounts of education during the antebellum period—though they continued to trail educationally advanced communities such as Salem.

The information on enrollment, attendance, length of public school year, and the amount of education received per child indicates that Beverly was making important gains in the two decades before the Civil War though it had not caught up with school systems in communities such as Salem which were also progressing during these same years. This analysis suggests that in the antebellum period Beverly citizens were working hard to upgrade public education in their community and a higher proportion was sending children to school than ever before. If the people of Beverly did not respond enthusiastically to the creation of a public high school, they at least sought to provide public education for everyone at the common school level.

SCHOOL EXPENDITURES

While most historians of education have focused on the amount of schooling received by antebellum children, nineteenth-century parents and taxpayers often were more concerned with the costs of that education and who should pay for it. Many of the problems caused by differences in educational opportunities among Massachusetts communities stem from inequalities in the tax bases which supported local education. Moreover, we can only understand the reactions of the citizens of Beverly to the proposed high school in the context of the overall cost of public education in that community.

The cost of public schools in Beverly rose in real dollars (1860 = 100) from $2,717.88 in 1840 to $6,152.56 in 1860—a huge increase of 126.4 percent. The citizens of Beverly had responded to the pleas of Horace Mann and local citizens for improved public education by a major increase in spending for that system. Thus, in evaluating the support or lack of support for education in Beverly, we need to remember that the taxpayers of that community supported a major expansion of that system during the two decades before the Civil War even though it meant increasing per capita costs of public education in real dollars from $.59 to $1.04—an impressive increase of 76.3 percent.[11]

The citizens of Beverly accepted a higher rate of per capita taxation to fund the expansion of public school education—but did this occur within the context of a general expansion of the economy and how did their expenditures compare with those of their counterparts in other cities in the Commonwealth? To answer these questions, we can calculate the amount of school expenditures, public and private, per $1,000 of valuation of taxable property. This will give us some indication of the relative economic burden of education in the antebellum period.

Although the per capita costs of public education soared in Beverly, the overall cost of public and private education as a share of taxable property in that community declined from $3.84 to $2.30 per $1,000 of valuation (see figure 2.6). It is important to observe that while Beverly lagged behind Salem in the length of the public school year and the annual number of days of school per person under twenty, it usually spent a larger proportion of its taxable wealth for educational purposes than Salem did. In other words, while Beverly does not seem as committed to education as Salem if we look only at the indices of the amount of education supplied and received in each community, the picture is just the reverse if we look at the relative economic ability of each town to finance education.

As we note the decline in the total school expenditures in Beverly as a percentage of taxable wealth, we may be surprised by the opposition of many taxpayers to the establishment of a public high school. Yet another perspective on this issue may provide some clues to the concerns of the taxpayers. The overall school expenditures per $1,000 valuation declined, but the share of public school expenditures significantly increased while that of private school expenditures decreased. Public school expenditures rose from $1.70 per $1,000 valuation in 1839–40 to $2.15 per

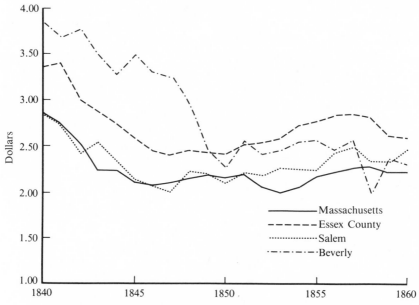

Figure 2.6. School Expenditures per $1,000 of Valuation, 1840–60

$1,000 valuation in 1859–60—an overall increase of 26.5 percent.[12] Thus, though the relative economic burden of education in Beverly decreased for the families with school-age children since those costs were now shared by even those who had no children in school, it significantly increased for Beverly taxpayers as a whole.

The relative burden of public expenditures in Beverly was considerably higher than in Salem. In 1839–40, Beverly taxpayers spent 60.4 percent more per $1,000 valuation than their Salem neighbors; in 1859–60 the Beverly taxpayers still spent 33.5 percent more per $1,000 valuation than Salem residents spent.[13] Thus, given the relatively more limited economic base of Beverly compared to Salem, its citizens were more financially supportive of public education than would be suggested by simply looking at the overall amount of money spent on public or private education in those towns.

As mentioned earlier, the per capita costs of education rose dramatically in the twenty years prior to the Civil War. Was the community's growing investment in public education unusual or did it simply parallel increases in other municipal expenditures? To pursue this issue, Beverly municipal expenditures per 100 persons (adjusted for the cost of living) were calculated at five-year intervals from 1800 to 1860 from the town budgets (see table 2.1).[14]

Table 2.1. Beverly Municipal Expenditures in Dollars per 100 Persons, Adjusted for Cost of Living (1860 = 100)

Year	Poor	Schools	Highways	Abatements	Officials	Fire	Health	Military	Incidental	Total
1800	16.45	19.30	19.18	12.62	5.16	.24	4.14	.66	12.25	90.00
1805	17.91	22.68	45.81	27.22	7.73	7.84	.12	1.03	3.98	134.31
1810	14.35	26.26	18.74	14.53	2.42	.11	.07	2.85	2.88	82.22
1815	21.89	23.09	14.02	21.48	2.14	.27	.07	1.96	5.84	90.77
1820	20.19	25.99	8.40	17.13	4.91	.98	.23	.07	2.00	79.89
1825	15.00	29.64	22.49	18.39	3.30	13.40	.24	.57	3.67	106.70
1830	26.09	44.01	12.09	23.69	3.54	2.54	.64	1.85	7.23	121.68
1835	27.77	43.64	39.98	21.91	3.88	6.00	.98	.69	10.45	155.31
1840	24.63	57.96	55.02	29.40	4.20	3.28	4.73	1.34	11.99	192.56
1845	34.45	73.38	25.87	43.96	6.50	33.13	20.04	0	34.43	271.75
1850	35.95	67.18	47.25	21.59	9.48	10.26	11.86	0	12.19	215.75
1855	70.54	108.38	115.40	27.62	8.61	17.10	11.27	0	20.39	279.31
1860	89.92	99.98	55.53	5.63	15.02	54.20	21.00	7.72	19.11	368.12

Source: Calculated from Town of Beverly Auditors' Annual Reports and U.S. Censuses from 1800-60. The cost of living adjustment data are from Paul A. David and Peter Solar, "A Bicentenary Contribution to the History of the Cost of Living in America," *Research in Economic History* 2 (1977): 1-80.

Beverly public school expenditures increased from $19.30 per 100 in 1800 to $99.98 in 1860—an astounding increase of more than 400 percent. Municipal expenditures for other services also increased during these years, but at a somewhat slower pace than for public education. Public schools accounted for 21.5 percent of Beverly expenditures in 1800 and 27.2 percent in 1860. In the two decades prior to the Civil War, however, there was relatively little change in the proportion of money spent on public education in Beverly.

The proportion of municipal funds spent in Beverly on public education was almost the same in 1860 as in other Essex County communities, urban (Lawrence, Lynn, and Salem) or rural (Boxford, Hamilton, Lynnfield, Topsfield, and Wenham). The total amount of money spent per 100 individuals in the rural communities was slightly less than in Beverly but considerably more in the urban areas.[15]

Thus, while per capita public school expenditures in Beverly did increase significantly in the decades prior to the Civil War, they were still less than those in larger and more affluent urban areas such as Lawrence, Lynn, and Salem. Per capita public school expenditures grew at about the same pace as municipal services in general in Beverly in the twenty years prior to the Civil War—suggesting that the citizens' willingness to finance more schooling was part of a more general trend toward increasing public services in the antebellum period rather than a unique concentration on expanding education.[16]

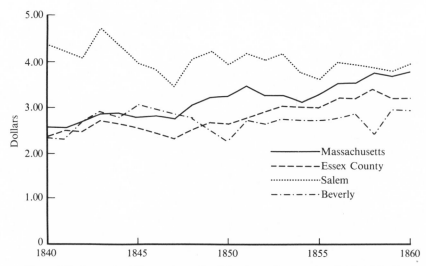

Figure 2.7. Amount of Money Spent for Schools per Person, Age 0–19, 1840–60

Up to now we have considered school expenses from the perspective of the community and the taxpayers. Now we will look at the costs of education from the point of view of the students to see whether the quality of their education, as indexed by the expenditures, may have shifted over time.

In terms of public and private expenditures, in real dollars, per person under twenty, Beverly spent more money on education over time (see figure 2.7). In 1839–40, Beverly spent $2.34 per person under twenty on education; in 1859–60 it spent $2.93 per person under twenty—or an increase of 25.2 percent. While Salem was cutting back on the amount of money on education spent per person under twenty, Beverly increased its support—though Salem's expenditures remained higher and by 1860 Salem was still spending a third more than Beverly spent.

In the years between 1840 and 1860 as Beverly shifted away from private schooling, the amount of public expenditure per person under twenty increased even more rapidly (see figure 2.8). While the town spent only $1.03 per person under twenty for public education in 1839–40, by 1859–60 that figure had risen to $2.74—a large rate of increase of 166.0 percent during those years.

It is also important to compare developments in public school expenditures in Salem and Beverly. Although Salem spent considerably more money on public school education per person under twenty in 1839–40, Beverly not only caught up with Salem, but surpassed it by 1859–60. The overall amount of money, public and private, spent per person under twenty in 1859–60, however, continued to be much higher in Salem than in Beverly because in Salem private education still accounted for 34.1

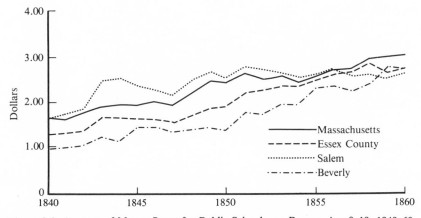

Figure 2.8. Amount of Money Spent for Public Schools per Person, Age 0–19, 1840–60

percent of total school expenditures while in Beverly it accounted for only 6.5 percent of total school expenditures.[17]

Although Beverly citizens spent considerably more on education per person under twenty just before the Civil War than it had two decades earlier, this does not necessarily mean that the amount of money spent per pupil increased since Beverly schools enrolled an increasing proportion of persons under twenty and since the schools were kept open longer. The increased expenditures may have been used almost exclusively to fund the expansion of the system.

To see whether the quality of education, as indexed by expenditures, may have changed over time, we can calculate the cost (in real dollars) per 100 days of school (see figure 2.9). In Beverly, there was relatively little change. In 1839–40, the cost per 100 days of school attended was $3.96 and had declined to $3.73 by 1859–60. A similar decline, though more marked, occurred in Salem. So we see that the increase in the overall amount of money spent per person under twenty in antebellum Beverly did not result in more money being spent per day of schooling actually received.

While the overall cost per 100 days of education changed relatively little in Beverly, the cost of public schools greatly increased—from $2.33 per 100 days in 1839–40 to $3.64 in 1859–60 (see figure 2.10). The increase in the cost of public schooling by more than 50 percent reflects to a large degree the community's willingness and need to pay more for teachers (salaries constituted most of the school budget).[18] While one cannot and

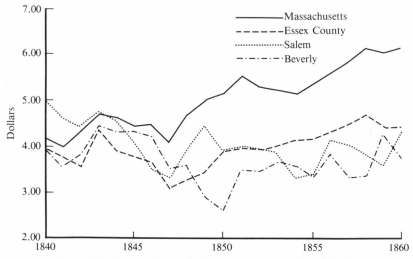

Figure 2.9. Cost per Hundred Days of School Attended, 1840–60

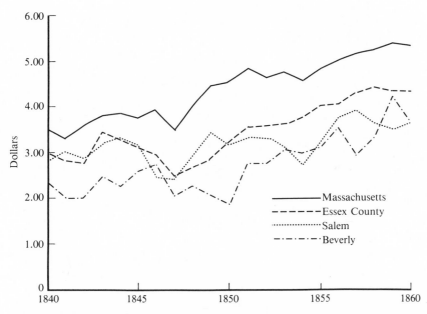

Figure 2.10. Cost per Hundred Days of Public School Attended, 1840–60

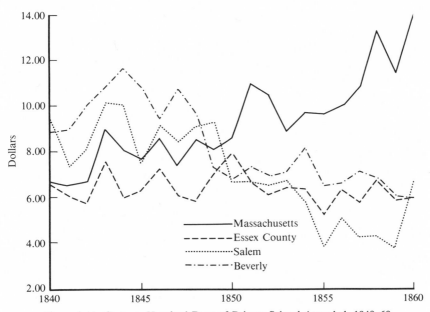

Figure 2.11. Cost per Hundred Days of Private School Attended, 1840–60

should not equate rising costs with increases in educational quality, it may be that the caliber of teachers hired in Beverly during these years was improving.[19]

While the cost of public education rose, the cost of private education declined from $8.82 per 100 days of school in 1839–40 to $5.99 per 100 days of school in 1859–60 (see figure 2.11). Since this decline in the cost of school occurred at the same time that fewer and fewer students were attending private schools, the total amount of money available for private schools dropped dramatically—thus perhaps reducing the quality of teachers willing to work in private as opposed to public schools. One result of this shift probably was to make public education increasingly attractive in Beverly compared to private education and thus further encourage parents to send their children to the public schools.

DIFFERENCES IN SCHOOL ATTENDANCE AND EXPENDITURES AMONG LOCAL SCHOOL DISTRICTS IN BEVERLY

One of the major shortcomings of the current analyses of antebellum education is that they have focused almost exclusively on large urban school systems such as Boston, New York City, or Philadelphia and have paid relatively little attention to small communities such as Beverly or rural areas such as Boxford or Lynnfield.[20] Furthermore, the few studies which have analyzed educational developments in smaller communities, such as Katz's analysis of Beverly, have usually ignored the differences among the local school districts within that town.[21] Yet reformers such as Horace Mann devoted much of their attention and rhetoric to the problems caused by the inequities among local school districts and urged that these be eliminated or at least reduced by a more centralized town school system. According to the antebellum reformers, differences in educational opportunities for children within the same community were often larger than those within the state as a whole. Unfortunately, historians of antebellum education have yet to pursue this matter in any detail and instead implicitly treat the communities in most studies as homogeneous entities in terms of education.

In order to see just how similar or dissimilar the educational opportunities and experiences were within small antebellum Massachusetts communities, we will investigate in some detail the variations in the provision of education in the nine local school districts of Beverly in 1857–58—the year in which the public high school was debated and established.

Although Beverly at that time was a relatively small community with about six thousand inhabitants, it was subdivided into nine public school districts, each maintaining its own separate schools. The size of a district's population had a major impact on the type of education that could be offered. The populations varied greatly and ranged from 341 children between the ages of five and fifteen in the largest district (Grammar) to 18 children in the smallest (Dodge's Row). The average number of children ages five to fifteen in those districts was 127 but six of the nine districts had fewer than one hundred children.[22]

As a result of this great disparity in the populations of the districts, the number of pupils enrolled in each of the public schools also varied greatly. For example, while the average daily attendance in the winter schools of 1857–58 in the Grammar district was 230, it was only 17 in both the Bald Hill and Dodge's Row districts. Although three of the nine districts (Grammar, South, and Cove) had an average daily attendance of more than one hundred pupils in the winter public schools in 1857-58, the rest had fewer than sixty-five scholars attending.

The impact of these differences on the quality and quantity of available education is very important. Dodge's Row and Bald Hill districts each taught their pupils in a single classroom. Students in Grammar, South, and Cove districts had a choice of attending a grammar, an intermediate, or a primary school depending upon their age and knowledge. While more specialized training was not necessarily better (despite antebellum reformers' advocacy of it), it did provide for more varied courses—especially in the upper levels. Children in the early primary grades may have received very similar instruction in all nine districts, but the older students in the larger districts had more access to subjects such as physical geography, natural philosophy, algebra, geometry, physiology, astronomy, Latin, and French. For example, about 7 percent of the students in the three largest school districts were taking algebra, but fewer than 1 percent of those in the three smallest ones were pursuing that subject. Moreover, children taking the higher branches of learning in the larger districts could expect to do so with other classmates, those in the smaller ones had to do so by themselves.

The percentage of school-age children attending school generally was not much higher in the larger districts than in the smaller ones; nor was attendance necessarily any more regular in the larger districts than in the smaller ones. But the number of days of schooling available to children was considerably greater in the larger districts. Schools in the large Grammar district operated almost year-round while those in the smaller districts were kept open only eight to nine months. As a result, the number of days of public school education received per child ages five to fifteen was usually much higher in the larger districts (see table 2.2).

Most of the inequality in the amount and type of education available

Table 2.2. Number of Days of Public School per Child, Age 5-15, in Beverly School Districts, 1857-58

School District	Total Number of Students	Number of Days of Public School per Child, Age 5-15
Grammar	363	173 (178)
South	240	137 (143)
Cove	246	130 (159)
Washington	112	136 (173)
Bass River	102	97 (110)
East Farms	121	116 (152)
West Farms	82	125 (164)
Bald Hill	53	59 (93)
Dodge's Row	28	150 (192)

Source: Calculated from the Beverly School Committee, *Annual Report for 1857-58.*
Note: Figures in parentheses indicate the total number of days in public school per child, age 5-15, including those attending under age 5 or above age 15.

to children in Beverly was due to variations in the financial resources of the local school districts. Public school funds were raised in part by means of a poll tax and initially were apportioned strictly on the basis of the number of polls in each district. The problem of unequal resources arose because the number of taxable citizens varied from district to district. In 1843-44 the number ranged from 340 in the Grammar district to 25 in Dodge's Row. That year Dodge's Row received only $47.50 for its entire school budget, while the Grammar district had $646.00.[23]

In part, of course, the differences in money allocated reflected differentials in the number of students to be taught, but there were still serious inequalities. While the average amount of money allocated per public school student in Dodge's Row was only $1.90 in 1843-44, it was $6.46 in the Grammar district.[24] This represented not only an inequity in the amount of money allocated per student, but also in the absolute amount of money available to hire teachers. Economies of scale allowed the larger districts to keep schools open longer and to hire better teachers.

In 1843-44 the outlying districts registered complaints about the inequalities in this system. The town responded by showing that the small districts were receiving a fair share of the funds considering the number of tax dollars they contributed to the town coffers.[25] Although this was true, it did not solve the problem of inequalities due to size. Therefore, in 1845 the town abandoned its practice of appropriating school funds on the basis of taxable polls and shifted to a system where one-eighth of the public school funds would be equally divided among the districts and the rest would be allocated on the basis of the school-age population.[26] This did not eliminate the problem, but it reduced it to some degree. In 1854 the formula again was changed so that 20 percent of the money for the common schools was apportioned equally among the districts and the rest distributed on the basis of the number of school-age children in each of the districts.[27] Thus, there were continuing debates within Beverly over the distribution of funds to the local school districts with the smaller ones gradually receiving a larger share of the resources.

By 1857–58, the amount spent per student was actually greater in the smaller school districts than in larger districts (see table 2.3)—a major improvement over the early 1840s. The total amount of available resources still varied among districts because of the differences in the number of school-aged children within them so that children in the Grammar district, as we have already noted, received more and probably better instruction than their counterparts in districts such as Dodge's Row and Bald Hill.

The inequalities in the amount and type of instruction available in these public school districts were compounded by the quality of the school houses in which the instruction occurred. Again, the differences in the value of the public school houses per children ages five to fifteen were not always very large (see table 2.3). But the economies of scale associated with the larger school districts meant that pupils attending public school in the Grammar district, for example, were instructed in buildings altogether worth $7,000 in 1857–58 while those in Dodge's Row district pursued their course of studies in a $75 building. Furthermore,

Table 2.3. Expenditures for Public Schools in Beverly School Districts, 1857–58

School District	Total Number of Students	Expenditure per Child, Age 5–15 (dollars)	Total Expenditure (dollars)
Grammar	363	4.20	1,433.72
South	240	4.35	1,049.72
Cove	246	4.53	806.83
Washington	112	5.30	445.31
Bass River	102	5.41	422.23
East Farms	121	5.17	476.08
West Farms	82	6.34	310.70
Bald Hill	53	5.79	364.54
Dodge's Row	28	10.64	191.47
Total	1,347	4.81	5,500.00

Source: Calculated from Beverly School Committee, *Annual Report for 1857–58.*

Table 2.4. Condition of Public School Houses in Beverly School Districts, 1857–58

School District	Total Number of Students	Value of School House (dollars)	Year Built	Value Per Student Attending (dollars)
Grammar	363	7,000	1857	19.28
South	240	3,750	1847	15.63
Cove	246	3,700	1853	15.04
Washington	112	1,200	1830	10.71
Bass River	102	1,400	1842	13.73
East Farms	121	1,400	1837	11.57
West Farms	82	2,200	1857	26.83
Bald Hill	53	700	1818	13.21
Dodge's Row	28	75	1813	2.68
Total	1,347	21,425		15.91

Source: Calculated from Beverly School Committee, *Annual Report for 1857-58.*

the public school houses in the larger districts tended to be much newer and presumably better built, while those in the smaller districts such as Dodge's Row or Bald Hill were constructed in 1813 and 1818 respectively (see table 2.4).

The differences among the Beverly school districts in the amount and type of education offered to their students are very important for any understanding of the debates over the Beverly Public High School in the 1850s. Katz minimized the importance of geographic differences among those who voted on the public high school question. As we shall see in the later chapters, however, these differences were quite important in understanding how people responded to this issue.[28] Many of the parents and taxpayers in the larger school districts such as Grammar favored a public high school as the next logical extension of the diversified type of education that already was being provided for their children. Their counterparts in the smaller districts saw the public high school as an unnecessary luxury since their own children still did not receive as good an education as children elsewhere in the community. Rather than spend additional tax dollars on a public high school which their children were not likely to attend, they favored using the money on the common schools in the smaller districts. In fact, after several of the early votes went against a public high school, the town voted to spend the amount of money that had been proposed for the high school on the common schools. Thus, the differences among the local school districts in the amount and type of education they offered played an important role in how voters as parents and taxpayers responded to the Beverly High School.

EDUCATIONAL INNOVATIONS AND CONTROL
OF THE PUBLIC SCHOOLS

In most antebellum Massachusetts communities, there was considerable tension, even animosity between the town school committee and some of the prudential committees of the local school districts over such issues as the hiring of school teachers, the distribution of school funds, and the adoption of educational innovations. These struggles were among the most important factors in the adoption or rejection of educational reforms, yet historians have all but ignored them in their analyses. In fact, though Katz analyzes in great detail the fight over the establishment of the Beverly Public High School in the late 1850s, he does not even acknowledge the equally acrimonious struggles over the control of the town's public schools—even though these debates significantly shaped and influenced the reactions of the townspeople to the high school.[29]

Since the town school committee was elected in a town meeting, the residents from the more populous areas such as Grammar or South districts, theoretically might have been able to pack the committee with persons interested in maintaining the advantage held by the larger and wealthier school districts, even if it were done at the continued expense of the smaller and poorer districts, by minimally responding to the more general educational reforms urged by Horace Mann and others. But in Beverly, as in many other Massachusetts communities, this was not the case. The town school committee, much more than any of the local prudential committees, was concerned for the well-being of all of the town's school children, not just those from the most settled areas. Although many of the actions of the town school committee, such as the call for a public high school, benefited the larger districts more than the smaller ones, others, such as the change in the formula for distributing school funds spread the benefits in the reverse pattern. Furthermore, it was the town school committee rather than the prudential committees which pressed for the adoption of almost all of the educational reforms and improvements in Beverly—sometimes in the face of determined opposition from the rest of the citizens. An examination of the characteristics and motivations of the men who composed the Beverly School Committee will enable us to understand better the dynamics of educational change in that community.

In his analysis of education in Beverly, Katz also considers the roles played by some school committee members in the creation and defense of the Beverly Public High School. He singles out Robert S. Rantoul, Sr., a long-time member of the Beverly School Committee, as the leader of the effort to establish a public high school in that community. Katz portrays

Rantoul's longing for the social harmony of the past and Rantoul's fear of the consequences of the economic transformation of Beverly in the 1850s as important factors in his support for a public high school. He traces Rantoul's career in great detail, documenting his involvement in the commercial life and industrial development of Beverly because Katz sees in this background the key to understanding Rantoul's interest in educational reform. The relationship between the business background of education promoters and the reform process is central to Katz's explanation not only of educational developments in Beverly, but elsewhere in the Commonwealth, stating: "As in Beverly, the school promoters throughout Massachusetts were people intimately connected with the economic transformation of the State."[30]

While Katz is correct in stressing the efforts of men such as Robert Rantoul, Sr., in promoting education in Beverly and elsewhere, he has given us a very narrow and quite misleading picture of them and has exaggerated their influence in this effort. Rantoul was, as Katz emphasizes, very involved in the commercial sector of the economy, first as an apothecary and then as a wealthy investor and participant in other ventures such as the Marine Insurance Company. But Rantoul was equally active throughout his life as a social reformer. Rantoul was a leader in Massachusetts of many social reforms: the abolition of capital punishment, the temperance movement, the peace movement, and the abolition of slavery. He served for fifty years as a member of the Beverly Overseers of the Poor and performed many other civic duties, all consistent with and evidence of his philosophy that each individual has a responsibility to serve his fellow man and his community. Indeed, throughout Rantoul's writings and career, one is continually reminded of his strong commitment to public service:

> I recommend it to my grand children to avail themselves of opportunities of public usefulness in humble spheres. Many who despise small things, pass through life looking for opportunities to undertake great things, which not finding they suffer very much mortification and disappointment, which would have been prevented by endeavoring to do the good which from time to time presented itself, heartily and truly, however small it might seem in the eyes of the unreflecting. Let it be a maxim to do promptly and earnestly the duty that at the time presents itself; not waiting for great occasions, which rarely are found by those who seek them.[31]

By omitting this aspect of Rantoul's character, Katz does not present a very balanced or accurate picture of what may have motivated Rantoul to strive for a public high school in Beverly. By overstressing Rantoul's fear of economic dislocation as the source of his support for the Beverly High School, a fear which Katz cannot document directly but about which he can offer only conjecture, Katz misses the more general humanitarian and reformist impulse that played a key role in guiding Rantoul's life and behavior. Furthermore, Rantoul participated in the various reform efforts from a very early age—well before the threats of the economic transformation of Beverly, as portrayed by Katz, might have prompted him to action. Rantoul, like Horace Mann, saw nothing incompatible in his efforts to promote commercial and industrial development, his efforts to alleviate the sufferings of others, and his attempts to bolster the existing capitalist system.[32] By focusing upon only one aspect of the lives of reformers such as Rantoul, Katz and many other historians of education have not provided us with a very complete understanding of the complexities of the motivations of antebellum school reformers.

A fundamental weakness in Katz's analysis of the politics of Beverly school reform is his lack of a systematic investigation into the background of the Beverly School Committee members. By focusing on only three individuals, Robert Rantoul, Sr., Dr. Wyatt C. Boyden, and William Thorndike, Katz presents a misleading description of the composition of the town school committee—one that distorts the role of the clergy in Beverly:

> Often the ministry played an active role, but in most towns lay participation was important and critical. For many years one of the most active educational reformers in Beverly was William Thorndike, a rich merchant. And so it was throughout the commonwealth. The supporters of education wrote the legislation, invested the money, and ran the enterprises that brought about the economic and social transformation of Massachusetts.[33]

Robert S. Rantoul, Sr., and Wyatt C. Boyden were unusually active members of the Beverly School Committee and served altogether twenty-three terms in the period 1841–1860 (occupying 9.9 percent of the positions during those years). But William Thorndike's leadership occurred well before the last two decades of the antebellum period, as he died in 1835 at the age of forty. What Katz fails to point out is that during the two decades before the Civil War when a public high school was being considered, Christopher T. Thayer, a minister, was repeatedly chosen as the chairman of the Beverly School Committee. In fact, of the sixty-seven different individuals who served on the Beverly School Committee from 1841 to 1860, twenty-three, or 34.3 percent, were ministers. The role of the ministers on the Beverly School Committee becomes even more prominent when we discover that they held 46.1 percent of the available seats during that twenty-year period. Indeed, with only a few exceptions every minister in Beverly in the two decades prior to the Civil War served almost every year on the School Committee.[34] Thus, not only were ministers by far the single most represented occupation on the Beverly School Board, they were also more likely to be reelected to that position than their lay counterparts.

It is difficult to know exactly what prompted each of the Beverly clergymen to devote so much of their time and energy to the public schools. For a few, such as Rev. Edwin Stone of the Second Congregational Church, the expansion and improvement of public education was a primary goal. Whenever possible, Stone championed public education for improving individual character and functioning while at the same time furthering the well-being of society as a whole. In an address before the Essex County Agricultural Society in 1845, Stone observed:

It is the Mind that gives man his supremacy. It is developed intellect that lifts one man above another, and procures for the individual unblest with this world's abundance, respect, honor, influence and consideration that wealth can never purchase. I would give him a fair start in the world—a fair chance to be felt, through the influence of his talents, in the assembly of his townsmen, or in the halls of legislation. I would have every farmer's son know enough of chemistry, to analyze soils, and prepare composts—enough of geology, to understand the origin and nature of soils—enough of botany, to understand the structure of plants and flowers, and to classify them—enough of natural history, to know the habits of the animal, feathered and insect tribes—and enough of physiology, to recognize the laws of health, and the secret of prolonged life. In a word, I would have him a perfect master of his noble calling, so far as depends on education. And it is for this reason, that I desire to see our Common Schools, where the majority of our children, and nearly every farmer's son receives his entire education, fostered with increasing care, and made equal to the highest intellectual cultivation that stops short of the University. I insist upon this high standard, because intelligent labor is better and cheaper for those who hire, than ignorant,—because I wish to see agriculture placed in its true position before the world, and dignified in the eyes of its own sons—because I would banish forever the false notion, that physical toil is incompatible with intellectual culture—and because I would not have withdrawn from the plough, one ray of the glory that encircled it, when Cincinnatus quitted it to command the Roman Armies, or our own Washington, to be the Saviour of his Country.[35]

Stone's paean on behalf of schooling for the sons of farmers was not just a thinly disguised endorsement of education as a means of furthering commercial agricultural development, but part of a more general call for universal education. In the same address, he advocated equal education for females:

> In my plea for education, I can make no distinction in the sexes that God has not made. I believe the best education, and the fullest development of their intellectual powers, that circumstances will permit, is the right of both,—of the sister as much as the brother. If knowledge is a blessing to the latter, it can be nothing less to the former. The purpose of female education, as is justly remarked by a successful female educator, is to lead the sex in the path of duty— to make better daughters, wives and mothers—and better to qualify them for usefulness in every path within the sphere of their exertions. The true object of education, is not to lead woman from her own proper sphere, but to qualify her for the better discharge of those duties which be within it.[36]

Stone's enthusiastic visions of the benefits of learning and his tireless efforts on behalf of education may not have been shared by most other Beverly ministers, but his speeches and writings do illustrate the close connection between common school reforms of the antebellum period and the activities of certain Protestant clergymen.[37] Perhaps more typical of the role of the clergy in educational reform is that of the above-mentioned Rev. Christopher Thayer of the Unitarian Church who viewed his long service on behalf of public education as just another facet of his service to youth in general rather than a reflection of a special commitment to public schooling. For him, as for many other Protestant ministers, service to the community, especially in areas such as education, was considered a normal part of his duties in the antebellum period:

> It may justly be expected of every Christian pastor to watch and labor especially for the young. No part of the care devolved on me has been more cheerfully and assiduously executed than this, whether it was to be exercised for them in or out of their homes, on the sabbath or the weekday, in the private or public schools, which last—as from my coming here, one year excepted, I have been a member of the General Committee, and, most of that period, its chairman—have claimed and received a large share of my time and attention. But, for whatever it may have been in my power so to do

for the young, I have been richly rewarded by their friendship; and yet more by what I have witnessed of their progress in knowledge, virtue, and preparation for future usefulness, honor, and happiness.[38]

Throughout the debates on educational reforms, including the establishment of a public high school, we shall find that the clergy, as well as a few particularly active individuals such as Rantoul and Boyden, played key roles.[39] Indeed, because of their aggressive insistence on educational changes and expansion, the ministers and their immediate allies on the Beverly School Committee were sometimes singled out in the 1850s for special retaliation by their opponents in the town meetings. Figure 2.12 shows the proportion of the Beverly School Committee who were ministers in the pre-Civil War period. In the period 1841–49 56.6 percent of the Beverly School Committee seats were occupied by ministers, but from 1850–60, the portion of seats held by ministers was only 37.3 percent. In 1855 and 1856 the percentage of clergymen on the committee plummeted because the opponents of the educational changes advocated by the Beverly School Committee were able to deny nearly all of the clergymen their traditional seats.

With very few exceptions, the members of the Beverly School Committee in the two decades before the Civil War pushed for the expansion and improvement of education in that community. In this effort they were greatly influenced by the annual suggestions from the secretary of the Massachusetts Board of Education. Throughout this period major policy innovations suggested by Horace Mann and his successors at the state level often were quickly accepted by the Beverly School Committee and

Figure 2.12. Percentage of Beverly High School Committee Members
Who Were Ministers, 1841-60

recommended for adoption by the citizenry at the next town meeting. In assessing the impact of Horace Mann on educational changes in the Commonwealth, historians will need to devote more attention to the diffusion of his reform proposals and consider in detail the catalytic role of his annual reports and speaking tours across the state.

An illustration of the close connection between the suggestions of the secretary of the Massachusetts Board of Education and their adoption by local communities is provided by the change in the formula for distributing public school money in Beverly. Before 1845 each local school district in Beverly received its share of the public school money on the basis of the number of ratable polls in each district. As we pointed out in the previous section, this procedure seriously handicapped the small, outlying districts like Bald Hill and Dodge's Row which did not receive enough money to hire good teachers or to keep their public schools open year round.

In the required annual town reports to the state in 1843-44, Horace Mann requested each community to relate its method of distributing tax revenues among the local districts. He used the returns in his Eighth Annual Report (for 1844-45) to plead for a more equitable distribution of funds either by changing each town's existing method of allocation, or even better, by not dividing the town into individual school districts but by treating them as a whole.[40] While Beverly was unwilling to go so far as to eliminate local school districts, it did adopt a resolution introduced by Robert Rantoul, Sr., for "a more liberal appropriation to the small districts" which stated that "one eighth part of the money raised for schools shall hereafter be equally divided among the ten school districts, and that the residue of the sum raised shall be divided among the said districts in proportion to the number of persons between the ages of four and sixteen in the respective districts."[41] Since the residents of Beverly had debated in previous town meetings the equity of the distribution of town services among the different areas, they were prepared to respond favorably to Rantoul's motion to reformulate the way public school funds were distributed. Thus, local circumstances were joined with the stimulus from the secretary of the Massachusetts Board of Education via members of the Beverly School Committee to effect a major change in the way public schools were funded in that community.

On many issues of educational improvements, such as the redistribution of public school funds, the purchase of the Common School Journal for the district schools, the creation of school libraries, and increasing aid for public schools, the Beverly School Committee and the citizens attending the annual meetings of the town could agree without too much debate or dissension; on other issues, such as the questions of the maintenance of districts, the control over the hiring of teachers, and the establishment of a public high school, the town was deeply divided. While the Beverly School Committee generally favored centralizing the control of education in its own hands, many of the citizens, spurred on by the members of the prudential committees of the local school districts, jealously resisted any such efforts.

During the 1840s the Beverly School Committee sought to upgrade the quality of education and, as we have seen earlier, made creditable gains in that direction. Although the committee reports sometimes described the shortcomings in the then present system of public schools, their general tone was both optimistic and self-congratulatory. When Rev. Edwin M. Stone resigned from the Beverly School Committee because he had accepted a pulpit in Providence, Rhode Island, he sent a letter to the Beverly town meeting which exemplifies the tone of the local school committee members in the 1840s:

> Nearly thirteen years have lapsed since I became a citizen of Beverly. During twelve of these years, by favor of my fellow Townsmen, I have held a seat at the School Committee's Board. Early interested in the cause of Common Schools, the duties of my office have been among the most agreeable to my public life; & it has been a source of constantly increased satisfaction to witness the steady advancement of popular education in this town. Our School Houses, now, without exception, are neat and commodious—the standard of qualifications in Teachers, is in accordance with the most elevated views of the times—the relation of parents & guardians to the schools is better understood—the evils of irregular attendance are gradually diminishing,—and the improving moral character of pupils is highly encouraging.
>
> I by no means intend to intimate, that our Public Schools, are as perfect, as they may or should be; but I am free to say, that they have never before stood as well, the recent examinations as a whole, evinced, a thoroughness in teaching,—a progress on the part of the pupils,—and spirit in the Districts, surpassing all former years.[42]

Although the 1840s witnessed a few clashes between school promoters and the citizens of Beverly, including an unsuccessful attempt to create a public high school in 1845, any negative effects of these controversies seemed short-lived. There is no indication, for instance, of any concerted effort, such as occurred later in the town meetings, to dismiss members of the School Committee because of their positions on particular issues. Perhaps this relative harmony was a result of the general agreement between the Beverly School Committee and the citizens on the need for educational expansion and improvement of the common schools as well as the mild manner in which the school committee persisted in its efforts to achieve its goals.

For some as yet unknown reason, a major change in the tone, tactics, and even in some of the goals of the Beverly School Committee took place in the early 1850s. Although there was no major change in membership, the school committee that was elected in 1852 adopted a much more militant and strident attitude about the need to improve the Beverly public schools. Gone was the self-congratulatory tone of the earlier reports. Instead, the new school committee questioned the efficacy of the then present school system and was especially critical of the training and inexperience of the teachers and the lack of a superintendent:

> The School Committee would respectfully submit to the Town that in their opinion, our common schools, under the usual management do not accomplish all of the good of which they are capable. This deficiency arises in part from the inequality of teachers. Most of our teachers pursue their business, only for a limited period, and not as a profession. They are mostly young men pursuing their own education at our Literary Institutions. Our schools, therefore, are subject to all the evils, arising from the irregularities of character attainments and experience of these temporary teachers. The duties of the committee are arduous, and difficult to be performed, requiring an amount of attention, labor and devotedness to the subject which it is difficult for them to render. Their own professional avocations are sufficient to occupy their time—and if perfectly qualified they could scarcely do justice to the schools, even if paid for their services. The committee would therefore earnestly recommend that the Town authorize the Committee to employ a suitable Superintendent of the Schools to perform these services and pay him a reasonable compensation for his labor.[43]

At the same meeting that had elected this more determined school committee, the town voted to set up a committee of fifteen residents, chosen at large, but including at least one from each school district, to look into the possibility of abolishing the present school district system. The members of this new committee consisted of most of the current members of the Beverly School Committee as well as others who had been active in school affairs earlier.[44]

At the next town meeting in March 1853, the committee of fifteen reported that it thought it was not expedient at that time to abolish the existing school district system, but it did recommend that the power of selecting and contracting with the teachers of all of the public schools should be placed in the hands of the town school committee rather than the local prudential committees—a reform that had been strenuously urged by the secretary of the Massachusetts State Board of Education. The town meeting disagreed with this recommendation and voted to continue to allow the respective prudential committees to select and contract with their own public school teachers. The meeting did, however, after some debate, agree to allow the school committee to hire a superintendent.[45]

The school committee that was elected at the 1853 meeting continued the new activism initiated by its predecessor. It distributed to all families a circular which covered topics such as constant and punctual attendance, preparation of lessons out of school, attention to all the prescribed studies, continuance of children at school, visiting the school by parents, and other ways of promoting the effectiveness of the schools. It also printed, for the first time, a very long school report and had it circulated to each family. In that report the school committee, undaunted by the negative vote at the previous town meeting, again called for a transfer of the power of hiring teachers to the school committee from the prudential committees.[46]

The people at the town meeting of March 1854 were no more inclined to give the power of hiring teachers to the school committee than those at previous town meetings had been, but they inadvertently neglected to pass a resolution specifically giving that power to the prudential committees.[47] As a result, by default, the school committee for the first time assumed the power of hiring all of the public school teachers. According to the school committee accounts, this was a highly successful experiment that should be repeated.[48] The citizens at the next town meeting, however, did not share the committee's enthusiasm for the new procedure—especially since many people felt that they had been deliberately tricked by the school committee. A motion, soon withdrawn, was made to withold the pay of the teachers who had been contracted by the school committee during the previous year. In any case, those at the town meeting moved quickly to shore up the decentralized educational structure long traditional to Beverly. They reauthorized the prudential committees to hire all teachers in the future, continued the school district system, rejected the creation of a public high school, and voted out of office nearly two-thirds of the then current members of the School Committee—a deliberate purging of those who the voters felt had betrayed their trust and who continued to seek the centralization of the educational system within the town.[49] Thus, we see accented by this series of votes the growing linkage between the movement to establish a public high school and broader efforts at educational reform such as changing the district school system and shifting control of the hiring of school teachers from the prudential committees to the school committee.

3 / Establishment of the Public High School in Beverly

THE story of the public high school in Beverly consists of three parts —the events leading to its creation in 1858, its abolition two years later, and its reestablishment the next year. Katz's analysis focuses heavily upon the abolition of the high school and simply assumes that those who favored its continuance in 1860 were also the ones who championed its establishment in the 1840s and 1850s.[1] As we shall see, this is not always the case since some of those who voted for it in 1858 and 1860 did so only because of a court indictment against the town. Furthermore, while Katz goes to great lengths to emphasize the extent and significance of the opposition to the Beverly Public High School in 1860, he totally ignores the fact that it was quickly reestablished the very next year.

This chapter will investigate the creation of the Beverly Public High School. Katz presents a wide variety of reasons cited by Massachusetts educators for establishing public high schools in the Commonwealth, but he devotes surprisingly little attention to the sequence of events leading to the creation of the Beverly High School. While he attempts to document the argument that socioeconomic turmoil in that community during the 1850s led local leaders such as Robert Rantoul, Sr., and Wyatt C. Boyden to call for the creation of a public high school, Katz tells us very little about its actual origins. Indeed, the reader would never know from Katz's account that efforts to establish a public high school in Beverly originated in the early 1840s rather than the 1850s. Furthermore, his cross-sectional correlation analyses of the factors associated with the presence or absence of a public high school in some Massachusetts towns in 1840 and 1865 are flawed methodologically and do not address the issues of the establishment dates and relative geographic locations of the early public high schools in the Commonwealth.[2]

In a sense the impulse for a high school in Beverly, Massachusetts can be traced back to colonial times. Massachusetts was an early leader among the colonies in establishing schooling beyond the elementary level, as evidenced by its famous law of 1647 which required all towns with a population of one hundred families or more to maintain a Latin grammar school. The eight Commonwealth communities that were initially affected by this legislation complied with it, but many other communities tried to ignore it as their populations surpassed one hundred families in the eighteenth century.[3] In 1789 the law was changed to make the establishment of a grammar school mandatory only if the community contained two hundred or more families, thus eliminating the legal requirement for such schools among the smaller communities.[4]

Beverly established a grammar school in 1700, as did many other Massachusetts communities, and employed a series of teachers, often for very short terms, to staff it. In 1782 the town briefly discontinued the grammar school but was forced by the Court of Sessions to reopen it. In 1824, however, the provisions of the 1789 legislation regarding the maintenance of grammar schools were changed so that towns with fewer than 5,000 inhabitants were no longer required to support them. The citizens of Beverly promptly abandoned the town's grammar school—displaying an indifference or hostility toward public education beyond the elementary level that would continue to characterize much of the community for the next three decades.[5]

The abolition of the requirement to maintain grammar schools was followed three years later by new legislation which required many communities to establish one of two types of high schools. This 1827 statute, which is quoted here at length because of its importance, formed the basis for all subsequent legislation on public high schools in Massachusetts and played an important role in the efforts to create such an institution in Beverly in the 1840s and 1850s:

> Be it enacted by the Senate and House of Representatives in General Court assembled and by the authority of the same. That each town or district within this Commonwealth, containing fifty families, or householders, shall be provided with a teacher or teachers, of good morals, to instruct children in orthography, reading, writing, English grammar, geography, arithmetic, and good behavior, for such term of time as shall be equivalent to six months for one school each year; and every town or district containing one

hundred families or householders, shall be provided with such teacher or teachers, for such term of time as shall be equivalent to eighteen months, for one school in each year. And every city, town, or district, containing five hundred families, or householders, shall be provided with such teacher or teachers for such term of time as shall be equivalent to twenty-four months, for one school in each year, and shall also be provided with a master of good morals, competent to instruct, in addition to the branches of learning aforesaid, the history of the United States, bookkeeping by single entry, geometry, surveying, and algebra; and shall employ such master to instruct a school, in such city, town, or district for the benefit of all the inhabitants thereof, at least ten months in each year, exclusive of vacations, in such convenient place, or alternately at such places in such city, town, or district, as said inhabitants, at their meeting in March, or April, annually, shall determine; and in every city, or town, containing four thousand inhabitants, such master shall be competent in addition to all the foregoing branches, to instruct the Latin and Greek languages, history, rhetoric, and logic.[6]

The 1827 legislation created a new legal framework for the establishment of schooling beyond the elementary level. The old Latin grammar schools were no longer mandatory for any community. Instead, towns with at least five hundred families were now required to create an upper-level public school which would teach American history, bookkeeping, geometry, surveying, and algebra, and only those cities with more than 5,000 inhabitants would be obliged to teach Latin and Greek. In other words, the Commonwealth moved away from its limited system of mandatory grammar schools, which were intended to prepare students for college, to a broader system of lower- and upper-level public high schools which provided more practical and commercial education. While these early public high schools in Massachusetts varied somewhat in organization and curriculum, there was in them a shift away from exclusive preparation for college toward more general education—in many ways replicating the approach of the then flourishing private academies scattered throughout the Commonwealth.[7]

There was no single or precise definition in the antebellum period of what constituted a public high school. High schools tended to be publicly supported and controlled institutions whose services were available to all the inhabitants of the community and which emphasized training in the subjects enumerated in the 1827 legislation. In most communities the high school tried to provide, under various organizational schemes, training for those planning to go to college as well as for those interested only in pursuing a more immediate, commercial career. With the growing diversity of education being offered in the common schools, the high school was in many communities the logical next step in education for older students. Public high schools seemed particularly appropriate for those areas which had high concentrations of students and which were already subdividing their pupil populations into specialized classes. While ages and preparation requirements for admission to public high schools varied across the Commonwealth, most systems set a minimum age such as twelve and required evidence of a certain level of academic proficiency.[8]

Previous to the enactment of the law, public high schools had been established in only two communities and another two (or possibly three) acquired them in 1827. As it turned out, the officials of the Commonwealth were generally reluctant to enforce the 1827 legislation, and in 1829 another law made it optional for towns of five hundred or more families to maintain high schools, so by 1835 only four other communities had established public high schools.[9] Thus, despite the passage of a comprehensive law in 1827 that called for the creation of lower and upper public high schools throughout the state, only a few communities did so.

As mentioned previously, the citizens of Beverly quickly abolished their grammar school in 1825 following the repeal of the legislation that had made it mandatory. Therefore it is not surprising that the town did not build a public high school even though it should have according to the 1827 legislation. Indeed, Salem (1827) and Newburyport (1831) were the only two Essex County towns to establish high schools before 1835 even though eight others, including Beverly, were required to do so according to the new law.

Instead, a group of thirteen leading citizens of Beverly, including some of those most active on behalf of public education, banded together to establish a private school in 1833 under the direction of Abiel Abbot of Wilton, New Hampshire, as principal and Mary R. Peabody as his assistant. In 1835 this school was incorporated as the Beverly Academy.[10] Since many of these and subsequent trustees of the Beverly Academy later became vocal supporters of the need for a public high school, one might surmise that these original proprietors of the Beverly Academy would have preferred establishing a public institution rather than investing their own resources in a private academy but despaired of convincing their fellow townsmen to establish a public high school at that time.

The decision of a group of Beverly citizens to incorporate a private academy in 1833 was not unusual in the Commonwealth. In fact, be-

Table 3.1. Incorporation of Academies in Massachusetts, 1780–1875

Date	Number
1780–85	5
1786–90	1
1791–95	7
1796–1800	4
1801–05	7
1806–10	4
1811–15	2
1816–20	6
1821–25	4
1826–30	28
1831–35	32
1836–40	14
1841–45	11
1846–50	10
1851–55	14
1856–60	5
1861–65	4
1866–70	6
1871–75	5
Total	169

Source: Alexander James Inglis, *The Rise of the High School in Massachusetts* (New York: Teachers College, 1911), p. 11.

tween 1831 and 1835 the largest number of new incorporated private academies in the Commonwealth were created (see table 3.1). This suggests that while many individuals were eager to send their children to secondary schools in the late 1820s and early 1830s, they found it difficult to convince their neighbors of the need to spend public funds for secondary education despite the passage of the 1827 legislation.

The Beverly Academy continued in operation until November 1854 when Issachar Lefavor, the principal and new owner of the academy building since 1848, left to accept a position as the principal of the Ipswich Grammar School.[11] During the approximately twenty years of its operation, the Beverly Academy attracted about thirty to forty students each year who altogether paid approximately $800 to $900 in tuition annually to receive an extension of their common school education or some classical training. During the whole period that the Beverly School Committee was making determined and continued efforts to convince the town of the need for a public high school in the 1840s and 1850s, it spoke approvingly of the Beverly Academy as "an excellent institution," in "good condition," and "very flourishing."[12] Although the presence of the Beverly Academy may have lessened the need for a public high school in the minds of some townspeople, its example and success encouraged others, including many of its proprietors, to continue the effort to convince the citizens of that community to erect a public high school.

The Revised Statute of 1835 repealed the 1829 act which had exempted communities from establishing a public high school and fully reinstated the provisions of the original law of 1827.[13] As a result of the repeal of the 1829 exemption as well as the growing crusade for educational reform throughout the Commonwealth, seventeen new public high schools were created between 1835 and 1839—almost twice as many as had previously existed.

In Essex County public high schools were established in three additional communities—Ipswich (1836), Marblehead (1837), and Gloucester (1838). During the debates over the creation of these high schools, the legal requirements for them were frequently cited by their supporters. For example, the Gloucester School Committee Report for 1838-39 cited section five of the 1827 law which required the town to maintain a public high school and it chastised the other members of this community not only for ignoring that requirement, but for trying to evade it by pretending that each district school was a town grammar school. After reminding their fellow townsmen of the heavy financial penalty for not complying with the 1827 legislation, the authors of the Gloucester School Committee Report went on to state the case for a public high school:

> The question whether the town be not really liable to twice the highest sum ever raised for the schools, by neglecting to provide for a town school, is a question of very little consequence compared with the manner in which the character of the town is implicated by any covert attempt to evade the law, or compared with the vital interests of our children left unprovided for.
>
> That all education, beyond the mere rudiments of learning taught in the district schools, ought to be confined to the families of a few fortunate citizens who can afford to send their children out of town to school, is a proposition so aristocratical and justly odious, that it would not be listened to for a moment; yet such is the practical consequence of the neglect, on the part of the town, to provide higher schools. Unless it is for the interest of this town that the great mass of the next generation should grow up in comparative ignorance, while the most arduous efforts are making, in every part of the State, to elevate and improve our Common School Education, this crying evil calls aloud for a remedy. The committee

conceive that they have done their duty in calling the attention of their fellow-citizens to this subject. It now remains for the town to do theirs. (A town school has since been established).[14]

In the early 1840s, the rate of establishing public high schools slowed due to the enactment of a law in 1840 which provided "that any town now required by law to maintain such a school as described by the fifth section of the twenty-third chapter of the Revised Statutes, shall be released from their obligation by raising and expending annually for the support of town or district schools, twenty-five per cent. more than the greatest sum ever raised by assessment by said town, for this object, before the passage of this act, anything in said section to the contrary notwithstanding."[15] As a result, only nine new public high schools were created in the Commonwealth from 1840 to 1847 when this exemption was finally repealed. Furthermore, some of the high schools that had been established earlier were dismantled during this period as the exemption gave the towns a new, legal means of evading the requirement to maintain a public high school.

By the early 1840s, six communities in Essex County had established public high schools—including Haverhill which acquired one in 1841.[16] Of the five largest towns, four now had public high schools (Lynn, the second largest town, had only a private incorporated academy). Five other Essex County communities, including Beverly, which were required by the 1827 legislation to maintain a public high school in 1840 did not—some of them were exempt from the requirement by the fact that they were spending more money on the common schools.

Although Beverly had a "flourishing" private academy at that time, Frederick W. Choate and others petitioned the town on March 1, 1844, to establish a public high school. After a lengthy debate at the annual town meeting, the town rejected the petition. Reacting to the arguments of the supporters of the high school that Beverly was not in compliance with the law, the town voted "that the Selectmen appropriate the money raised for schools which is hereby voted to be twenty five percent additional in amount to any sum raised by the town prior to 1840 among the several school districts according to the several rated polls therein."[17]

Several pertinent observations can be made about the events in Beverly in 1844. First, even though Katz implied that the movement to establish a public high school in Beverly began in the 1850s as a reaction to the growing social and economic tensions within the community, the actions taken at this meeting show the movement's origins actually go back to at least a decade earlier. Second, though Katz minimized the importance of state legislation in influencing the efforts to establish high schools, in truth the proponents of the public high school relied heavily on the requirement of a high school as stated in the 1827 legislation to bolster their case for such an institution. These arguments did not result directly in a high school, but they had sufficient impact at the town meeting in 1844 to induce the residents to raise town school expenditures 25 percent above the 1840 level in order to be legally exempt from the 1827 legislative mandate. Finally, it is important to note that the majority of those attending the Beverly town meeting in 1844 rejected establishing a school and chose instead to spend their additional funds for the common school. This allocation problem, involving a deliberate tradeoff between improving common schools and establishing a public high school, is a recurring theme in the debates in Beverly between the outlying, smaller districts eager to obtain more funds for their common schools, which were woefully understaffed and in need of repairs, and the larger districts, recipients of most of the existing public school budget, which wanted an expansion of the existing public school system including the establishment of a public high school.

Other towns beside Beverly had also taken advantage of the 1840 legislation exempting communities from establishing public high schools if they increased their educational expenditures by 25 percent. But this loophole was closed in 1848 when the law of 1840 was repealed.[18] Once again all Massachusetts communities were legally obligated to follow the 1827 statute. In addition, local support for high schools had greatly increased during the previous twenty years—at least among a small but important group of dedicated and zealous educational reformers. As a result of the renewed legal obligation to establish public high schools and the growing support for them among educational reformers at the local level, there was an increase in the number of towns establishing them. While the State Board of Education did not itself initiate judicial proceedings against recalcitrant communities, it did encourage its local supporters to take advantage of the more stringent regulations after 1848. Furthermore, in contrast to 20 years earlier when few of the school districts in the Commonwealth were ready for or needed public high schools to complete their educational offerings, residents of at least some of the more populous and developed portions of the larger communities now saw the value of providing a public high school education—especially since there was a growing feeling throughout the Commonwealth that public education was preferable to private education.[19]

The effect of repealing the 1840 legislation combined with growing local agitation, at least among some reformers, for public high schools can be seen in the large number of new institutions established after 1848 (see figure 3.1). The late 1840s and 1850s witnessed an unprecedented ex-

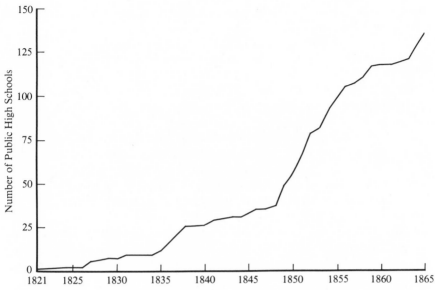

Figure 3.1. Cumulative Total of First Establishment of Public High Schools
in Massachusetts Towns, 1821–65

pansion of the number of public high schools throughout the Commonwealth.

The results of the change in the high school legislation are impressive.
Only 36.4 percent of the towns legally required to establish a high school
had done so by 1840, but that figure jumped to 55.3 percent by 1850, and
rose to 64.2 percent five years later (see table 3.2). By the end of the
1850s, nearly seven out of ten communities mandated to maintain a pub-

Table 3.2. Among Massachusetts Towns That Were Legally Required to Maintain Public
High Schools, Percentage Which Complied with the Law

Year	Percentage in Compliance
1830	8.6
1840	36.4
1850	55.3
1855	64.2
1860	67.2
1865	68.0

Source: Alexander James Inglis, *The Rise of the High School in Massachusetts* (New
York: Teachers College, 1911), p. 38.

lic high school had done so, as had another 16 towns that were not required to establish them.

The rapid state-wide expansion of public high schools is echoed by
developments in Essex County. In the 20 years after the 1827 legislation
only six public high schools had been built; in the next three years six
more institutions were created: Manchester (1848), Bradford (1849),
Lawrence (1849), Lynn (1849), Rockport (1849), and Danvers (1850).
Thus, by 1850 ten of the sixteen Essex County communities that were required to maintain public high schools had established them.

It might be expected that agitation for a public high school in Beverly
would have been renewed in the late 1840s, but, as mentioned in chapter
two, the Beverly School Committee was so preoccupied with other reforms and so satisfied with its achievements in improving common
school education that the issue of a public high school did not receive
much attention. In the early 1850s, however, a surge of educational
reform activity developed in Beverly. It focused first on the issues of hiring a full-time superintendent and reexamining the district system and
only later moved on to the issue of establishing a public high school.[20]
Thus, although educational supporters in Beverly pushed for more
reforms in the early 1850s, the establishment of a public high school was
not among their primary goals and certainly not their highest priority.
Yet the establishment of a public high school soon became the focus of a
struggle between a small group of educational reformers trying to enact
their view of a proper educational system and the rest of the citizenry
who saw the educational needs of the community differently.

At the March 1853 town meeting the voters decided to create the position of superintendent of schools and allotted $500 for that purpose; this
amount represented an increase of 12.5 percent over the existing school
budget.[21] The new superintendent, Rufus Putman, raised at the next
town meeting in 1854 the issue of limited opportunities for older children
in Beverly:

> And can it be that we are doing our duty to the scores of youth in
> our town, for whose education we are in an important respect ac-
> countable, while we withold from them the education which they
> need, and which many of them so earnestly desire? Is it doing all
> our duty to this class to furnish them with a teacher, for three or
> three and a half months in the whole year and give that teacher as
> much other labor as one man can possibly perform, without at-
> tempting to carry them forward in the higher branches of study?
> The fact that so many of the older scholars have attended the
> winter schools so regularly from the beginning to the end of the
> term, is sufficient proof, if we had no other, of the desire that exists

for a more thorough education than can be obtained under the present system.

It does not become me to express any opinion as to the best method of placing a more extended course of education within reach of those who are ready to avail themselves of the opportunity, were it provided. You, gentlemen, know better than I can, the best methods of supplying this want. The fact, however, that the school houses at which five sevenths of all the children in the town attend school are within a mile of a certain centre, and that that centre is accessible by railroad to one-seventh more, removes the objection which often exists, in towns of equal exent, to a central High School, open to all the youth of the town, whose age and literacy attainments may be deemed sufficient to give them admission to it.[22]

The call for the establishment of a high school by the new superintendent was certainly an important step in bringing this issue back before the town. We cannot tell, however, whether he was acting on his own or whether this was something that the rest of the members of the Beverly School Committee desired and wanted him to initiate. It seems doubtful that a new superintendent would have tried in his first year in office to raise this issue single-handedly unless he were assured of considerable support from the members of the town school committee as well as other community leaders. Furthermore, the sudden outpouring of support for this proposal in Beverly suggests that his effort was part of a well-coordinated plan among some Beverly citizens rather than just an isolated attempt by the new superintendent to provide for the needs of advanced students.

Another educational development was occurring at approximately the same time which may have furthered the cause of those wishing to establish a public high school. In November 1854 the private secondary school known as Beverly Academy was finally closed. The Beverly Academy had provided a place of education for older students in the community for over 20 years. Its closing in 1854, for whatever reasons, may have stimulated some Beverly citizens, especially those whose children were immediately affected, to join the effort to establish a public high school at that time. On the other hand, since private sources had provided an appropriate educational facility for interested parents and students for so many years, many other Beverly taxpayers may have felt that the town need not bear the costs of a replacement; if there was a demand for such an institution, one could be reestablished under similar private auspices without the aid of any public funds.

The campaign for a public high school was quickly taken up by the recently established local newspaper—the Beverly *Citizen*. On February 9, 1854, a month before the annual town meeting, it urged the creation of a public high school:

A High School. There is a very general feeling among our inhabitants in favor of establishing a High School in this town. A school of this description has been wanted for a number of years, for the accommodation of pupils who have advanced beyond the general standard of instruction afforded in the district schools. We believe there is no other town as large as Beverly in the State, which has not a High School—thereby affording to the youth an opportunity to prepare for college, or to pursue the higher branches of learning, without going out of town for that purpose. The present state of things with reference to this matter is certainly not very democratic. Our young men, under a truly democratic arrangement, who were desirous of proceeding in their studies beyond the ordinary standard, would be able to do so at a free High School. At the present, a young man, though very desirous of preparing himself for college, or for the study of a profession, would not be able to do so, under our free school system; and if his pecuniary resources would not enable him to pay his tuition at an academy, he would be obliged to give up his intentions. The want of a High School in this place may account for the fact that Beverly has not so many representatives in the learned professions as many other towns of the same size. This, however, is a matter of but little importance; but it is highly important that the youth of Beverly should be provided with all those educational advantages, which, under the laws of the state, they might justly claim for the public.[23]

Probably as part of a coordinated effort to create a public high school, Daniel Leach from the Massachusetts Board of Education was invited to address the citizens of the town two weeks before the annual town meeting on the best ways of promoting education. The issue of the high school was raised and apparently enthusiastically promoted since many of the staunchest supporters of the high school were present and active at that meeting.[24]

Daniel Hildreth and others offered a petition at the March 1854 town meeting calling for the establishment of a public high school. The town meeting referred the matter for investigation to a special committee of ten. The members of the committee were a diverse lot who generally had little previous experience in office holding in the community with only Rufus Putnam, the school superintendent, and Rev. Joseph Tracy representing the school committee. At the April 1854 town meeting, six

of the ten members, including both representatives of the school committee, presented a report favorable to the establishment of the high school.
After considerable discussion, the town voted against the proposal.[25]

Several observations can be made about the efforts in 1854 to create a
public high school. First, the attempt to establish a public high school
was part of a larger effort in the early 1850s to revitalize Beverly's school
system. As such, much of the impetus for this effort should be seen
within the broader context of educational reform—both in the origins of
that effort and in its importance. While the public high school was a very
important part of the reform agenda, it was only one of many other
reforms that were being advocated in that community. In fact, it is likely
that the educational reformers in Beverly attached more importance to
the abolition of the local school districts and to the hiring of a school
superintendent than to the building of a public high school.

Second, the renewed attempt to create a public high school in Beverly
should be viewed as part of the larger state-wide movement to build more
high schools spurred by the repeal of the 1840 exemption legislation in
1848. Instead of focusing exclusively on factors within Beverly that led
individuals there to want a high school, external developments such as
the changes in the legislation and the trend toward more high schools in
other communities in Essex County as well as in the rest of the Commonwealth should also be considered.

Third, though the new school superintendent played an important role
in calling for the establishment of a public high school, considerable
evidence suggests that this effort was part of a well-coordinated attempt
by many Beverly citizens rather than just the pet project of a new superintendent. Perhaps the idea of obtaining a school superintendent was
seen by some reformers only as the first phase of a more extensive plan to
reform the schools in Beverly.

Fourth, while Katz has made much of the role of Robert Rantoul, Sr.,
in the attempt to establish a public high school, there are reasons to
suspect that he played a very minor part by the time the crucial votes
were taken in 1854. Katz does not seem to be aware of a scandal which
was revealed in 1853 concerning the treatment of a Miss Maxey. Miss
Maxey was an insane person whose care had been supervised for many
years by the Overseers of the Poor in Beverly, a group whose membership included for many years Robert Rantoul. Miss Maxey was very
poorly cared for by the Board of Overseers who denied her the assistance
she needed. For its misconduct in this case, the entire Board of Overseers
was prosecuted by the town and forced to retire from office in disgrace.[26]
Although Rantoul was so highly respected for his past services to the
community that he was lavishly praised at the town meeting and in the

local newspaper (though not exonerated in the Maxey episode), he nonetheless sent a letter of resignation from all current or future town offices to the March 1854 town meeting.[27] In fact, at the meeting with Daniel Leach of the Massachusetts Board of Education which discussed educational reforms for the community, he does not appear to have been present.[28] In other words, though Katz devoted much attention to the ideology and role of Robert Rantoul in the fight for the Beverly High School, his actual level of influence and involvement in local affairs may have been seriously reduced just at the time when the issue of the high school was being decided.

Fifth, Beverly's clergymen made up one of the major groups urging a public high school as well as other educational reforms. As mentioned in the first chapter, clergymen routinely sat on the town school committee in larger numbers than any other group and many of them spearheaded the effort to establish the high school. Surprisingly, while Katz spent much time on the role of Rantoul, he entirely ignores the important role of the clergy in the process of educational reform.

Finally, though the decision in March 1860 to abolish the Beverly High School may have involved opposition to higher taxes for public education, the same was not true of the decision in April 1854. In fact, at the same town meeting at which the public high school was rejected, the citizens voted an additional $1,000 for the public schools—a sizable increase of 18.2 percent over the previous school budget.[29] Unlike the situation in 1844 when voting for such a sizable increase exempted the town from the obligation to maintain a public high school, in 1854 there was no such legal advantage to the town. Furthermore, while earlier town meetings had divided 12.5 percent of the general funds for schools equally among the ten districts and divided the rest on the basis of the school-age population, it was now decided to divide 20 percent of the general school funds among the districts and the remainder on the basis of the school-age population. Thus, as was true ten years earlier, the rejection of a public high school in Beverly was not a signal that the town had lost interest in public education, but an indication that the citizens of Beverly preferred to improve the quality of their common schools rather than build a central high school for a few of the older and more advanced students. The continued hostility to a public high school from the outlying local districts was also still evident. The smaller and less affluent districts gained substantially at this town meeting in 1854 not only by the expansion of the general school fund by nearly 20 percent, but also by the change in the formula for distributing those funds.

The defeat of the high school in 1854 as well as the rancor within the community over control of the local school districts formed a barrier which continued to frustrate efforts to establish that institution the following year. The Beverly School Committee, elected in 1854, advocated a public high school at its March 10, 1855, meeting:

> The chairman presented a paper, containing general remarks on the schools, and a recommendation to establish a high school which was adopted, as a portion of the committee's annual report to the town.[30]

But the town, outraged by legal but unauthorized actions taken earlier by that school committee, was of no mind to seriously entertain the idea of a public high school. As mentioned previously, in 1854 the town meeting inadvertently neglected to pass a resolution empowering the local prudential district school committees to hire their own teachers. The town school committee seized upon this technicality to hire, for the first time, all of the school teachers—even though it was quite clear that the town had never intended this drastic change in hiring procedures.[31]

Many of the citizens of Beverly were so infuriated by the town school committee, which they regarded as having usurped legitimate power and blatantly ignored the wishes of the townspeople, that for the first time no sitting member was reelected to the town school committee. Furthermore, though seven of the 11 members of the previous school committee had been ministers, none of the 12 members elected at the March 1855 town meeting were ministers.[32] Thus, the citizens of Beverly not only chastised the entire school board, but also evidenced a growing realization that the town could not rely upon these educational zealots, including the large contingent of ministers, to adequately take into consideration the interests of the town as a whole.

At the April 1855 meeting, 11 of the 12 school committee members who had been elected a month earlier resigned in order to show their displeasure at the wholesale removal of the members of the previous school committee. Their elected replacements included two of those chosen at the March meeting and five of the members from the previous school committee and signaled the attempt by the town to heal the wounds caused by the struggle over the control of the local districts.[33]

Despite the obvious move by most of those at the April 1855 town meeting toward a reconciliation, Robert Goodwin introduced a resolution that "the Town do not pay from any money appropriated the present year for school purposes any debts contracted by the School Committee the past year."[34] Although the motion was finally withdrawn, its introduction and debate, even after the compromise election of school committee replacements, suggests that a sizable group of Beverly citizens had not forgiven those educational reformers who had seized upon what most townspeople regarded as a technicality to try to dramatically change the control of local education.

During this attack upon the school committee elected in 1854, no effort was made to call for the establishment of a public high school which that now discredited group had endorsed. At a special town meeting in July 1855, called for the purpose of reacting to new legislation that authorized towns to purchase school books and stationery for their pupils, however, the proponents of the high school, led by David C. Foster of the school committee, succeeded in persuading the small number of people attending to endorse this change (by a vote of 45 to 22).[35] This decision continued to divide the town but was upheld the following year, and then decisively rescinded at the 1857 town meeting.[36] Thus, although the residents of Beverly had successfully defeated in 1855 the efforts of the previous school committee to control the hiring of teachers, the bitterness from that fight lingered and was intensified by the continued efforts of the newly elected compromise school committee and its small band of energetic allies to change the nature and control of public education in Beverly.

In the election of the school committee in March 1856 the town continued to try to reunite the factions of the earlier battles. Seven of the 13 members selected were part of the discredited school committee of 1854 and four of those were ministers.[37] Yet the educational issues dividing the town, especially with regard to the high school, continued to act as a wedge driving the sides apart. Rather than acknowledge that the continued hostility of the town towards a public high school was insurmountable and allow the passage of time to erase the bitter memories of the strife within the community over the high school, supporters of the high school insisted on reopening this matter at the next town meeting. Frederick W. Choate, newly elected chairman of the school committee as well as a returning member of the 1854 school committee, and others petitioned the town to establish a public high school. Once again, the petition was defeated.[38]

It is difficult to reconstruct exactly the next sequence of events because the town records suddenly became rather terse. It appears that after suffering two successive defeats on the establishment of the public high school, its supporters, still unable to accept the decision of the town meetings, threatened to invoke the Massachusetts state law requiring towns the size of Beverly to maintain a public high school. As a result, a special and unusual meeting of the town was called in December 1856 to deal with the issue of the high school. Despite the threat of court action, the townspeople once again rejected the motion to build a public high school.[39]

At the regular annual town meeting on March 1857, Joseph Ober, from one of the small school districts (East Farms), successfully offered a motion to repeal the authorization for the school committee to purchase books and stationery. At the same meeting, John I. Baker, considered to be the foremost political leader in the community, offered a motion which suggests that the threat of the town being taken to court was now regarded as a real possibility: "That the School Committee be authorized to establish a High School as required by law." His effort to bring Beverly into compliance with the state law was of no avail; the motion was defeated 145 to 213.[40]

At this point, the supporters of the high school went ahead with legal proceedings against the town. The next mention of this issue in the town records concerns a warrant for a future meeting in July 1857:

> To see what measures the town will adopt relative to an indictment again the town for nuisance, whether by defending the suit consequent thereon, or settling the same, or in any other manner deemed best for the interest of the town.[41]

The issue of the indictment against the town was discussed at the July 1857 meeting, but no definite action was taken. Perhaps the town hoped that by taking no official position immediately some form of compromise might be worked out.[42] In any case, it was necessary to call another town meeting on September 15, 1857, at which time it was voted that the selectmen be authorized to defend the interests of the town against the state.[43]

Having looked into the legal situation a bit further, the selectmen called for another town meeting on October 18, 1857, at which time they reported their findings:

> The 2d article of the warrant was then taken up, and after a statement by the Chairman of the Selectmen that he had consulted C. G. Loring Esq. and others upon the subject, who were all unanimously of the opinion that the town must establish a High School or suffer the penalty for their neglect.
>
> On a motion of William H. Lovett, it was voted. That the School Committee be authorized to establish a High School according to the law, and that a sum not exceeding four hundred dollars be appropriated for that purpose.
>
> 85 voting in favor and 79 in opposition to the above vote. An amendment to the above motion was adopted and after some discussions reconsidered.
>
> On the motion of Isaac Prince it was also voted That the School

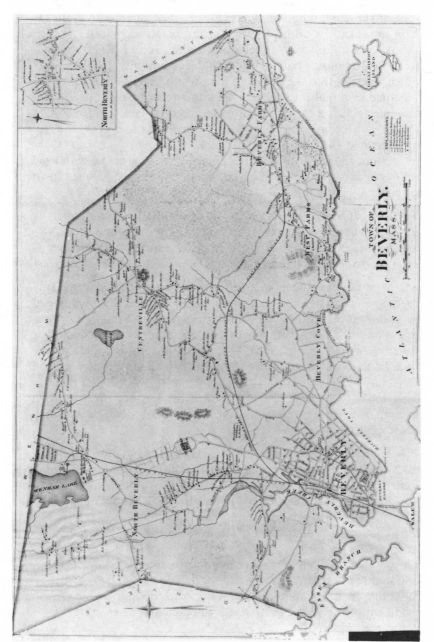

Figure 3.2. Map of Beverly

Committee locate the School at the Old West Farms School House
if the town is obliged to establish a School before March Meeting.[44]

Though Katz mentioned the indictment against the town for not complying with the state law requiring towns of the size of Beverly to have a
public high school, he failed to consider the implications of this important event. The majority of Beverly citizens never favored a public high
school—it was only passed when the unanimous opinion among their
lawyers made it clear that the town would not only have to establish a
high school, but pay a penalty as well for its delay. Even facing an indictment, a large proportion of the town was willing to incur the penalties
rather than give in to a minority of citizens who were using a state law to
circumvent the desires of the majority as expressed at the recent town
meetings. Thus, the high school was not an institution that was "imposed" on just the working class citizens of Beverly, but was imposed on
the large majority of individuals in that community who favored higher
taxes for common schools but not for a public high school.

A related factor which Katz ignored in his analysis of the later vote
against the Beverly High School in March 1860 was the tremendous
amount of bitterness that must have been generated by the imposition of
this institution on the citizenry in 1857. Many individuals, who may not
have been hostile to the high school per se, probably were outraged to
find a small minority of their townsmen continuing to try to subvert the
wishes of the majority by invoking a state law which had rarely been en-
forced in the courts. This use of state law also may have frightened
citizens from the outlying areas even more because by then they would
have realized that the minority in the town who favored a strong centralized school system might in the near future use some other newly
enacted state law to grab power from the local school districts despite the
wishes of the majority of taxpayers. In other words, to understand the
intensity and pattern of feelings against the high school in March 1860, it
is necessary to understand how it was originally created.

A second, more curious item in the vote to create the high school was
the amendment to have it placed in the West Farms district—one of the
smallest and least accessible areas of the community (see map of Beverly
in 1875). As the school report admitted after the creation of the high
school:

> During the winter term, with one or two changes, the number
> continued at 17. It appeared upon careful inquiry that the diminu-
> tion of the School at the fall term arose from the fact that the
> fatigue of daily travel to and from a part of the town so difficult to
> access, as the West Farms, was found upon trial to be too great for

many of those children who had at the outset hoped and endeavored to enjoy the advantages of this school.[45]

One might suppose that the locating the high school in the West Farms was done to obtain support for the high school from the outlying areas —but this does not appear to have been the case, especially since the individual who proposed that amendment was not noted as a supporter of the high school. Nor can the reason be that a large number of students from that area were particularly interested in attending the school since they did not do so once it opened. It is more likely that the opponents of the high school tried to retaliate against those who favored it and tried to limit support for it by locating it in an area that would not serve the majority of the town well. Perhaps, given the closeness of the vote at that meeting, the opponents thought that they might discourage enough supporters of the high school by putting it in such an undesirable location that it might even help to defeat the attempt to build the school. In any case, the location of the high school in the West Farms district meant that most children in Beverly had, at best, limited access to the facility. It may also be that the site selected symbolized the outrage felt by the majority of Beverly citizens over the manner in which they were forced to accede to that institution.

4 / Abolition of the Beverly Public High School in 1860

AFTER many years of struggle and a bitter final battle that pitted a determined minority of the town advocating a public high school against an angry majority opposed to it, the town of Beverly voted on October 18, 1857, to establish a high school at the old West Farms School House. Immediately following the vote, the Beverly School Committee met and appointed a subcommittee to prepare the rules and regulations for the governance of the high school. The school committee delayed contracting for the use of the Old West Farms School House, however, as there was strong feeling among the members of the school committee that this site was unsuitable because its location was inconvenient for most students. At the next town meeting, the effort to change the site for the new high school was strengthened by the fact that the district attorney, A. A. Abbott, consented to continue the indictment against Beverly to the May term of the Superior Court in Salem so the town did not need to establish the high school before the March town meeting in 1858.[1]

In preparing for the establishment of the public high school, the Beverly school Committee continued to extol the virtues of such an institution:

> Your committee are unanimous in the opinion that a High School of the first order should be immediately established, and that our children should have the full benefit of what may be called the completion of our excellent School Education. 1st, the Primary; 2d, the Grammar; and lastly, the High School; the three completing our unsurpassed School system.

Another reason for establishing a High School is, that we have not what many Towns possess, excellent Private Schools and Academies, into which many of our scholars might enter; we have nothing of the kind and it is to be hoped they never will be established in this Town, filled, as they generally are, by the children of wealthy parents, to the exclusion of the poor man's child. No, let us furnish the means of education to all, so that the children of the poor can have the same School privileges as do the children of rich men; can have the opportunity to make the same attainments, and fit themselves to occupy any and all stations in society to which they may aspire.[2]

The school committee also pointed to the benefits of the high school in encouraging older grammar school students to continue their studies in preparation for possible admittance to the high school. While some parents evidently had reservations about the need for advanced study or the ability of their children to master these subjects, the school committee did not. Indeed, the school committee confidently predicted that "our Schools can furnish one hundred, if not one hundred and fifty scholars, who can easily pass the examinations required for admission to this High School, or any other High School established in this State."[3]

The suspicion of many citizens of Beverly that the effort to create the high school was only part of a larger scheme to eliminate local school districts and to centralize the control of public education in the town was confirmed when the school committee observed:

It may not be improper, here to make a suggestion of this kind, that the Town should vote to abolish the District system, and purchase all the school houses belonging to the different Districts. The upper rooms of the Grammar District school house, might then be assigned for the accommodation of scholars, who might wish to attend the High school, which school would draw off from a part, if not all the Districts, the older and more advanced scholars, and in this way, the schools would be so relieved, that Female teachers might be engaged to take charge of a part of the schools, now taught by male teachers. Could this plan be perfected and carried out, a High school might be established, and maintained without entailing upon the Town much additional expense or lessening in any way the educational privileges now enjoyed by the scholars of the different districts. We would suggest that a large Committee be chosen, selected from every part of the Town, who should be entrusted with the sole control of our Public schools, with full power to grade them, as they might deem most for the interest of the Town.[4]

The March 1858 town meeting authorized the establishment of the public high school. Although the school committee had previously estimated that $1,500 would be needed for that institution, the town allocated $1,000. Furthermore, despite the clear indications that the West Farms area was not an ideal site for the high school, the town once again insisted that it be located there.[5]

The high school opened under the direction of John R. Baker on the first Monday in May and concluded the week ending March 5 with four weeks of vacation during August and one week at Thanksgiving. Candidates were required to be at least twelve-years-old, of good moral character, and to pass an examination in orthography, reading, writing, English grammar, modern geography, American history, and arithmetic. The school committee had anticipated that 100 to 150 scholars in Beverly would pass the entrance examinations and attend the high school. But only twenty-five girls and eight boys entered in May and that number diminished to seventeen "at the fall term . . . from the fact that the fatigue of daily travel to and from . . . the West Farms was found upon trial to be too great for many of those children who had at the outset hoped and endeavored to enjoy the advantages of this School."[6]

The small number of students entering the high school was a great disappointment to its supporters and was blamed, probably quite correctly, upon the insistence by the opponents of the institution that it be located at the West Farm. The Grammar district, which had the largest number of students in the town in its grammar school and had parents who were among those leading the fight for the high school, sent only four students; the West Farms district, which was much less supportive of the high school and had only half as many grammar school students, entered 9 students.[7]

Another indication that the creation of the high school had not settled the controversy is a statement from the school committee noting that one reason for poor attendance was "a certain feeling which we find to have pervaded the community to a considerable extent, and which has inevitably in some degree reached the School itself,—that the institution was standing upon an uncertain basis, that its permanence was doubtful—in short, that the town was rather playing at keeping High School, than keeping it in earnest."[8] Although the indictment against the town succeeded in establishing the high school, it could not ensure its successful or continuous operation as long as the majority of the citizens felt they had been unfairly coerced by a small minority of high school supporters.

At the March town meeting in 1859, Frederick Choate, one of the leaders of the high school movement, urged his fellow townsmen to allow it to be relocated in the Grammar district, but his motion lost by a 233 to 294 vote. Motions were then made to move it to other districts closer to the center of the town, but these were easily defeated as well. Failing to reach agreement, the meeting adjourned until the next day when another series of motions to improve the location of the high school were again defeated. Finally, Joseph Ober, an opponent of the high school, moved successfully to keep it at the West Farms in the same building as the previous year.[9]

The decision to keep the high school in the West Farms district discouraged any significant increase in enrollment. Only nine girls and three boys joined in the second year so that the total number of students was 17 girls and eight boys (even this number was reduced in the fall as inclement weather once again became an additional impediment).[10]

For many opponents of the high school, the low rates of enrollment only confirmed that there was no need for this institution—especially since per pupil the high school was very expensive compared to the primary or grammar schools. While the city spent $5.62 per student in the public primary and grammar schools, it spent $43.48 to educate each student in the high school during the 1858–59 school year. In addition, while the proponents of the high school had stressed its importance and value for preparing young men, nearly seven out of every ten students were female.[11]

The burden of maintaining a high school that had been forced upon an unwilling community by a minority became particularly heavy at this time due to the downturn in the economy after the Panic of 1857. This was especially true for two of the largest occupational groups in Beverly —the fishermen and shoeworkers. As the Beverly *Citizen* observed at the end of 1858:

> The Fisheries and the Boot and Shoe Manufactures are unquestionably among the most important branches of industry in this town, and, we may add, of this county. Both branches, we regret to state, have been unusually depressed during the past season. During the early part of the season, when the indications connected with our legitimate business were rather unfavorable, attention was very naturally directed to the fisheries, as the only alternative. But many who have braved the dangers and endured the fatigues of ocean life, have returned with the sad consciousness that they have toiled for nought, or have received but a meagre return for months of labor. Nearly all of our fleet have now returned, and comparatively few have succeeded; some have not even met their expenditures. A few only have secured large fares while the fleet, as a whole, have fallen considerably below the average of former years.[12]

The efforts to relocate the Beverly High School in 1859 failed and with them any chance for great increases in enrollments which might help to justify the cost of the high school. The poor economic prospects for a sizable portion of the Beverly community made the large expenditure of funds for the high school seem even less warranted. Thus, the controversy over the Beverly High School had not gone away and the announcement of the town meeting in March 1860 brought the entire matter before the taxpayers once again:

> To adopt such measures, grant such sums of money, and make such regulations in regard to the High School, and other schools throughout the town, and act and do anything respecting the same as they may deem expedient.[13]

Although there is no evidence that the opponents of the Beverly High School had caucused ahead of time, the backers of that institution, including the Beverly *Citizen,* sought to drum up support for it before the meeting. In a published letter to the editor, nine days before the town meeting, "A Looker On" praised the Beverly High School:

> This School is no longer an experiment of doubtful success if it ever was regarded in such a light. During the two years of its existence, it has gained a character of which it may well be proud. So far from proving a failure, it has accomplished much in the right direction. Though but few have enjoyed its advantages, yet the improvement made by those who have attended to its exercises, can but occasion no small regret that so many should have been deprived of such opportunities.[14]

It is interesting to note that even in praising the high school, the writer was forced to acknowledge that very few individuals had made use of it. Thus, although the parents of the children attending the high school might have been among its staunchest supporters, the importance of this factor was minimized because so few children were enrolled.

The townspeople met on March 12, 1860, and selected the officials for the coming year. Then they turned to a motion by Daniel Foster, one of the opponents of the high school, "that the town retain the School District System and that prudential Committees of the several School Districts be authorized to select and contract with the Teachers in the several School Districts for the ensuing year."[15] The motion carried and reaffirmed the desire of the town to keep the control of the public schools at the local district level rather than shift it to the town school committee.

As the town meeting did not complete its lengthy agenda that day, it adjourned and reconvened March 14, 1860. Frederick W. Choate, a strong supporter of the high school, moved that the high school should be located at the Armory Hall for the coming year. The motion was defeated.[16]

Joseph Thissell, a relatively wealthy shoemaker from the outlying Cove School district and part owner of a shop, then offered the following motion: "To discontinue the High School in this town and to request the Selectmen to secure disinterested legal counsel to carry the case to the Supreme Court if the case required it, and all Expenses to be paid by the Town Treasurer." After a series of parliamentary maneuvers, the vote was taken and it passed 249 to 143—the newly created Beverly Public High School had been abolished.[17] After adjourning for lunch, the town meeting reassembled and a motion to reconsider the vote on the high school lost 144 to 187.[18]

The unique feature of the vote to abolish the Beverly Public High School is that the name and vote of each of the 392 participants was recorded by the town clerk, John I. Baker. This highly unusual procedure was probably followed to emphasize the seriousness of the situation as well as to provide documentation for the town in the event this information was needed in the anticipated court case. It is the availability of this detailed voting information that has made the battle over the high school in Beverly so important to historians.

Following the general approach of Katz, as much information as possible was gathered on each of the 392 voters using the federal manuscript census, the town tax list of 1859, local church records, lists of organization officers in the Beverly *Citizen,* and the official town records. Complete information on age, nativity, occupation, wealth, children in the household, town municipal offices held, church membership, and location of residence was obtained for 370 of the 392 voters. Additional information on political affiliation and membership in various voluntary associations was gathered for subgroups of this population.[19]

Before turning to an analysis of the vote on the high school, it is useful to place it within a larger context. Although not everyone present at the town meeting answered the roll call, most voters probably did so.[20] Compared to most other town meetings, this one was unusually well attended. Nevertheless, not everyone in the town who was eligible to vote participated. In fact, only 25.6 percent of the ratable polls in Beverly cast a ballot. Katz has made much of this town meeting as a revolt of the working class, but the less affluent individuals were much less likely to have participated. While 32.8 percent of the polls with some property cast ballots, only 13.8 percent of those without any property voted.[21] Thus, although the issue of the Beverly High School attracted considerable attention compared to most other issues before the community, it did not bring out a majority of the citizens—especially compared to turnouts for state and national elections which usually attracted more than twice as many voters as the number that appeared on March 14, 1860, to decide the fate of the high school.

In analyzing the voting behavior of the individuals who participated, Katz used cross-tabulation. In other words, he simply calculated the percentage of voters opposed to the Beverly High School by some variable such as their wealth or occupation. Each independent variable (i.e., wealth, occupation, age, etc.) was cross-tabulated against the dependent variable (the vote on the Beverly High School).[22] The problem with this statistical approach is that it does not allow the analyst to make adequate inferences about the relative importance of each of the independent variables. Furthermore, Katz must have had difficulty in deciding the strength of the association between the variables in his contingency tables since he does not seem to have calculated any tests of the strength of those associations. Therefore, this analysis will use multiple classification analysis (MCA) because it permits the assessment of the relationship between each of the independent variables and the dependent variable while controlling the effects of the other independent variables.[23] Thus, it is possible not only to ascertain the relationship between a voter's position on the Beverly High School and his wealth separate from the effects of the other variables, but also the relative ability of one variable such as an individual's wealth, to predict his vote compared to the other characteristics of the voter.

Using contingency tables, Katz explored a variety of explanations of the voting behavior of the Beverly citizens on this issue. The problem throughout his analysis is that many of his independent variables are related to each other and it is difficult to untangle their relative importance using only cross-tabulation. Nevertheless, he succinctly summarized his findings:

> For three reasons, then, the Beverly citizens voted to abolish the high school: first, people, those without children especially, protested the raising of taxes; second, the least affluent citizens felt that the high school would not benefit their children; third, they were hostile both to the wealthy leaders of the town and to the onset of industrialism. The educational promoters, who were by and large the wealthy and prominent citizens, failed to preserve the high school because they advanced arguments unacceptable to the less prosperous citizens and because they overestimated their own powers of leadership. The supporters based their pro-high school arguments on mobility and economic growth; what they failed to see was that their own values were not shared by the entire community.[24]

In deciding what to include in the reanalysis of the vote on the Beverly High School, a large number of independent variables were considered. The final list consists of nine independent variables: age, nativity, children in the household, church membership, amount and type of wealth, occupation, town office holding, political affiliation, and geographic location. This includes all of the factors which Katz considered as well as the additional variables of church membership, town office holding, and political affiliation.

The age of the voter was used because the younger voters were expected to be more supportive of the high school than the older ones. The cohorts of individuals in their twenties and thirties, for example, grew up in a time when Horace Mann as well as his coworkers at the local level greatly stressed the value of educational reform. Older voters, on the other hand, grew up in a time when education was valued, but when the need for a high school education was not widespread and when it was expected that parents rather than the public should pay for any education beyond the common schools.

Katz found almost no differences in age between the supporters and opponents of the high school. This finding is confirmed in this study at the level of the simple relationship between the vote on the high school and the age of the voter since the eta^2 is very small (for this and all other references to the MCA, see tables 4.1 and 4.2). After controlling for the effects of the other factors, however, the age of the voter becomes much more important; younger voters were more likely to support the high school and older ones were more apt to oppose it. In fact, after control-

Table 4.1. Vote on the Beverly Public High School in 1860: Eta^2, Beta, Changes in R^2, and R^2

Variable	Eta^2	Beta	Changes in R^2 if Variable Removed
Age	.0100	.1331	− .0056
Nativity	.0023	.0661	− .0003
Children in household	.0031	.0715	+ .0018
Church membership	.0326	.0805	+ .0099
Amount and type of wealth	.0761	.2478	− .0384
Occupation	.0547	.0709	+ .0103
Town Officeholding (weighted)	.0886	.2783	− .0527
Political affiliation	.0618	.1277	− .0086
Geographic area	.1795	.3638	− .0847

Note: R^2 = .2952

Table 4.2. Vote on the Beverly Public High School in 1860: Class Means, Adjusted Means, Net Deviations, and Number of Cases (0 = Continue High School; 1 = Abolish High School)

	Class Mean	Adjusted Mean	Net Deviation	Number of Cases
Age				
20–29	60.0	54.4	− 8.0	83
30–39	63.0	61.8	− .6	78
40–49	60.0	63.7	+ 1.3	98
50–59	59.0	60.7	− 1.7	61
60 & above	74.0	76.3	+ 13.9	50
Nativity				
Born in Mass.	64.0	63.4	+ 1.0	337
Born elsewhere	52.0	52.2	− 10.2	33
Children in Household				
Older child in school	59.0	56.6	− 5.8	95
Older child not in school	66.0	63.3	+ .9	35
Only younger children	61.0	64.9	+ 2.5	111
No children	65.0	64.4	+ 2.0	129
Church Membership				
Unitarian	29.0	66.7	+ 4.3	14
2d Cong.	67.0	78.5	+ 16.1	6
Dane Street	63.0	59.0	− 3.4	40
4th Cong.	60.0	54.7	− 7.7	5
Washington	64.0	64.6	+ 2.2	14
1st Baptist	53.0	58.8	− 3.6	43
2d Baptist	93.0	71.8	+ 9.4	27
Other	62.0	61.9	− .5	221
Amount and type of wealth				
0	63.0	67.3	+ 4.9	71
$1–$999 (Maj. in R.E.)	70.0	64.7	+ 2.3	54
$1–$999 (Min. in R.E.)	52.0	57.0	− 5.4	58
$1,000–$4,999 (Maj. in R.E.)	77.0	72.9	+ 10.5	116
$1,000–$4,999 (Min. in R.E.)	50.0	48.2	− 14.2	36
$5,000 & Above (Maj. in R.E.)	47.0	56.5	− 5.9	15
$5,000 & Above (Min. in R.E.)	20.0	24.2	− 38.2	20

table continues on following page

Table 4.2. Vote on the Beverly Public High School in 1860: Class Means, Adjusted Means, Net Deviations, and Number of Cases (0 = Continue High School; 1 = Abolish High School) (continued)

	Class Mean	Adjusted Mean	Net Deviation	Number of Cases
Age				
Merchant	38.0	59.8	− 2.6	26
Manufacturer	50.0	57.6	− 4.8	12
Professional &				
white collar	36.0	61.7	− .7	36
Farmer	73.0	54.6	− 7.8	41
Shoemaker	72.0	63.7	+ 1.3	123
Fisherman, mariner	76.0	67.9	+ 5.5	29
Gentleman, no				
occupation	54.0	61.9	− .5	13
Other	61.0	64.3	+ 1.9	90
Town office-holding (weighted)				
0	70.0	68.4	+ 6.0	241
1	55.0	50.9	− 11.5	22
2	83.0	80.9	+ 18.5	18
3–5	52.0	45.1	− 17.3	29
6–9	56.0	68.5	+ 6.1	25
10–14	24.0	37.1	− 25.3	17
15 & above	17.0	22.1	− 40.3	18
Political affiliation				
Republican	28.0	43.8	− 18.3	36
Democrat	29.0	71.6	+ 9.2	7
Other	67.0	64.3	+ 1.9	327
Geographic area				
Bald Hill, East Farms				
West Farms	87.0	81.6	+ 19.2	47
Bass River, Dodge's Row,				
Washington	70.0	71.9	+ 9.5	56
Cove	94.0	87.9	+ 25.5	65
Grammar	42.0	44.7	− 17.7	149
South	51.0	54.2	− 8.2	53
Total	62.4			370

ling for the other factors, the age of the voter is the fourth best predictor of his position—better, for instance, than knowing the occupation of the voter. Thus, the advantage of controlling the other variables is nicely illustrated by this example since the age-cohort effects of the vote are lost if only class means are considered.

Initially, I expected to find strong differences between native-born and foreign-born voters, with the latter strongly opposing the high school since their children were less likely to use it. Unfortunately, since only about 8 percent of the town's population was foreign born and even a smaller proportion of immigrants than the native-born population attended the town meeting of March 14, 1860, it is impossible to pursue this distinction. Instead, the best one can do is to subdivide the population participating in the vote into those born in Massachusetts and those born outside the state (mindful that most of these were born in the United States).

Given the limitations of the data on nativity, no hypotheses seemed obvious. One possibility is that individuals born in Massachusetts would be more likely to support the high school because they grew up in a state particularly noted for its support of educational reforms. Perhaps some of these individuals also had been born and brought up in Beverly so that they were more attached to the community and therefore willing to invest in an institution which might enhance the town's image if not their own well-being (of course, the measure of nativity is so crude that it does not really allow us to test for this possibility with any degree of confidence). Yet the results indicate just the opposite—individuals born in Massachusetts were more likely to oppose the high school—even after controlling for the effects of the other independent variables. Furthermore, the nativity of the voter was the weakest explanatory variable overall and contributed very little toward predicting voting behavior.

There is no ready or obvious explanation for this pattern of voting behavior. Perhaps the individuals born in Massachusetts were more likely to be lifelong residents of Beverly and more traditionally oriented than those who had moved about during their lifetime in search of better economic opportunities. Again, given the great predominance of those born in Massachusetts and the lack of variation, this factor did not prove to be as interesting or useful a variable as was initially expected.

One of the three factors cited by Katz as most important in explaining how someone voted was the absence of children in the household. He found that a voter who had no children was less likely to support the high school, and he also found that among those who did have high school-age children, the number of such children made no difference in the voter's choice on the high school issue.[25]

In order to encapsulate the information on children in the household in a single variable, it was necessary to conceptualize the problem and operationalize the data somewhat differently than Katz has done. Rather than focusing on the numbers of children, except for those who had none, this investigation considered first the presence or absence of older children (and whether they went to school), and then the presence or absence of younger children in the household. In other words, the independent variable for this analysis first asks if there were any children ages 12 to 17 in the voter's household and then, if present, subdivides them into two categories according to whether any of these older children were in school. If there were no older children present, an effort was made to ascertain whether any children under age 12 were in that household.

The results generally support the direction and logic of Katz's earlier interpretation, but not the relative importance he attributed to this factor. As predicted, voters from households with no children were less likely to vote for continuing the high school. The presence in the voter's household of one or more older children enrolled in school increased the likelihood that the voter would support maintaining the high school—probably reflecting a generally more favorable attitude toward further education, or, perhaps even more specifically, the anticipation of sending one or more of these older children to the high school. If the household included older children but none was attending school, the voter was even more apt to oppose the high school than a voter who had no children—though controlling for the effects of the other variables considerably lessened this difference. Somewhat surprisingly, the absence of older children in the household but the presence of at least one child under age twelve did not incline voters, after controlling for the effects of the other factors, to support the high school. Perhaps this reflects the fact that many of the parents focused their attention on the common schools which their children were either attending or would soon be attending rather than on the high school which may have seemed so remote to their immediate needs that they ignored it. Overall, the variable measuring children in the household was only the seventh best predictor of voting behavior.

Many recent historians of education have had an unfortunate tendency to ignore the important role of religion in the expansion and reform of public education in the antebellum period.[26] Similarly, although Katz acknowledges that ministers participated in the public school reforms in the Commonwealth, he minimizes their exertions and emphasizes those of wealthy merchants and manufacturers.[27]

As discussed earlier, however, the Protestant ministers in Beverly did play a vital role in educational development in their community. Despite whatever theological differences that there may have been among them, the ministers banded together on behalf of educational expansion and reform in the decades before the Civil War. In the early 1850s, for example, representatives from all the churches in Beverly sat on the several different school boards which unanimously endorsed the establishment of a public high school and recommended other educational innovations. Indeed, the most striking feature of the clergy's support for education is that ministers from different denominations in Beverly continuously supported a public high school and other educational reforms even though there was a high rate of turnover of ministers in many of the churches.

The leadership role of the clergy in the establishment of the high school was acknowledged by the citizens of Beverly—but sometimes rather negatively by those opposed to that institution. Immediately after the defeat of the high school in 1860, a writer addressing the Beverly *Citizen* confirmed that the ministers had been singled out and derided at the town meeting for having forced the high school upon the community:

> The School Committee came in of course for the usual 'left hand' compliments; the Ministers especially! Though there were but four, of them, out of a Committee of twelve—still, as they have been the longest in the service, we suppose they were considered, on this account, the embodiment of all its sins. They were charged with having 'rid out the appropriations' and with 'ridding over the Town'! What a lucky circumstance that these clerical Jehus did not live in witch times![28]

Even though the ministers of Beverly championed the high school, their congregations did not necessarily agree with them on that issue. Indeed, given the resounding defeat of the high school as well as the apparently unchallenged criticisms of the clergymen at that town meeting, one can conclude that many parishioners voted against the recommendations of their spiritual leaders.

Since Katz did not discern the very important role of the religious leaders of the town in the establishment of the high school, it is not surprising that he did not try to ascertain the church membership of the voters—an imposing task given the considerable logistical difficulties involved in obtaining the records of the several different churches (few of these records are conveniently gathered together and deposited at one location). But because this reinterpretation of the fight over the Beverly High School assigns a larger role to the clergy, it seemed essential to reconstruct, as much as possible, the religious affiliation of the voters.

In 1860 Beverly had eight churches—all of them Protestant. Membership information was obtained from every church except the Universalist Church which was quite small at the time and probably was the place of worship for only two or three of the 392 voters at the March town meeting.[29] Thus it is possible to determine to what extent a clergyman's support for the high school was shared by his congregation.

A look at the simple percentages of the voters from each of the various churches supporting or opposing the high school shows a wide variation in the voting pattern among members of the different congregations. Percentages range from a low of 29.0 percent of the Unitarian voters opposing the high school to a high of 93.0 percent of the voters who were members of the Second Baptist Church being against it. Thus, although the clergymen unanimously supported the high school, their parishioners were not universally committed to it and some were barely interested. Perhaps the most surprising finding is that voters who were not members of one of these churches were actually a bit more likely to support the high school, after controlling for the effects of the other variables, than those who belonged to one of the seven churches.

When the variations in voting behavior by voters from the different congregations are examined some expected (as well as some unexpected) results emerge.[30] As anticipated, the simple percentages show the Unitarian voters to be the staunchest supporters of the high school with seven out of every ten endorsing the high school. This finding is consistent with other studies which have found that Unitarians such as Horace Mann were at the forefront of education reform in Massachusetts.[31] The Unitarians' commitment to the high school in Beverly is exemplified by the fact that their minister, Rev. Christopher T. Thayer, was one of the most prominent and active educational leaders in that community.

Therefore, it is surprising that when we go beyond the simple percentages and control for the effects of the other factors, we find that Unitarian voters were less likely to support the high school than others. This suggests that while Unitarians did support the high school, it was not because of their membership in that church or because of the influence of Thayer but because of other characteristics of the Unitarians such as where they lived, their wealth, or their pattern of office holding.[32]

The members of the Second and Fourth Congregational Churches worshiped in separate buildings and had different religious tenets but by 1860 they were drawing closer together theologically. When the original Second Congregational Church took on a more Unitarian theology during the 1820s and 1830s, a sizable portion of the congregation split off and formed the Fourth Congregational Church under Rev. John Foote. During the 1840s and 1850s, however, the Second Congregational Church lost members and had great difficulty in even maintaining a minister. Finally, in 1866 both congregations agreed to reunite under an Orthodox Congregational minister.[33]

Given the Unitarian orientation of the Second Congregational Church in the 1830s and 1840s, it might seem surprising that its voters were less supportive of the high school than those of the Fourth Congregational

Church. Yet this might simply be a further indication of the shift away from Unitarianism taking place by 1860 in the Second Congregational Church which made it possible for the two institutions to reunite after the Civil War.

The original members of the Washington Street Church were dissenters from the Third Congregational Church (Dane Street Church) who had left in 1837 due to disagreements over the use of alcoholic beverages by the Dane Street Church ministers and parishioners. The Washington Street Church had a very reformist bent: it took an early stand against slavery, was very rigorous and strict in its attitudes and doctrines on piety, and discouraged social events within the Church.[34] In addition to its strong temperance and antislavery leanings, the voters from the Washington Street Church, after controlling for the effects of the other variables, were found to be more opposed to the high school than their counterparts in the Dane Street Church who were less reformist, at least on the issue of temperance. This suggests that although enthusiasms of reformers often overlapped (an abolitionist might be a supporter of temperance or of public school expansion) the relationship did not follow a set pattern; the temperance-oriented Washington Street Church voters were not as supportive of the high school as their former brethren in the Dane Street Church.

The amount of support for the high school varied considerably among voters from the five different Congregational churches, especially between those who were members of the Congregational church with Unitarian ties and those who belonged to the others. Similarly, the behavior of the voters from the two Baptist churches differed significantly. Only 53.0 percent of the First Baptist Church voters were against the high school, while an overwhelming 93.0 percent of the voters of the Second Baptist Church opposed it. Some of this difference can be explained by the fact that the Second Baptist Church was located in the outlying East Farms section while the First Baptist Church was in the Grammar School district. But the voters from the Second Baptist Church still opposed the high school with greater frequency than those of the First Baptist Church even after controlling for the effects of geographic location as well as for the other factors in the independent variable list.

No single and simple explanation accounts for the particularly large number of voters from the Second Baptist Congregation who were against establishing a high school. To a large degree their opposition may have been part of the opposition shared by many of the other residents of East Beverly—a theme which will be explored later when geographic location is discussed as a factor in voting behavior. Their opposition may also have been influenced by the fact that the members of that society were especially hard-pressed financially in the late 1850s when they were trying to maintain their church under rather adverse conditions.[35] It does not seem, however, to reflect hostility to public education in general since the Second Baptist Church had for many years maintained a close and harmonious working relationship with the public schools in the East Farms district.[36]

Although it is difficult to account for some of the variations among the congregations in support for or opposition to the high school, the differences are sufficiently large to suggest that parishioners felt free to decline to echo the leadership of their ministers on the issue of educational reforms—especially when that advice conflicted with their other needs and interests. Overall, an individual's church membership is not a very strong predictor of that person's position on the high school. This finding simply reinforces the impression that although the residents of Beverly were willing to a large degree to delegate responsibility for educational affairs to their clergymen, they did not passively accept all of the clergy's policy recommendations—particularly when these entailed the expenditure of large sums of tax dollars on an institution that did not seem vital to the needs of the larger community.

According to Katz, one of the three most important factors in predicting support for or opposition to the high school was the amount and type of wealth possessed by the voter.[37] As he put it:

> Finally, the people who voted to abolish the high school were the least wealthy on every measure. Not only that but the distribution of the wealth they did have was different. Whereas those who supported the high school generally had an estate balanced fairly evenly between real and personal property, those who voted for abolition had more valuable real than personal holdings. That is, opposition to the high school came not only from the least wealthy but also from those whose holdings in land and buildings exceeded their personal property.[38]

The reasons for this pattern of voting are not entirely clear. On the one hand, the least affluent individuals presumably opposed the high school since their own children were unlikely to attend, whereas the wealthy supported it for their own children or as a means of stabilizing the community during this period of rapid socioeconomic transformation. On the other hand, as Katz also acknowledged, the wealthier individuals might have been expected to oppose the high school, as they would be paying most of the taxes for this institution and since most of them could easily afford to send their own children to a nearby private academy. Katz explains the large difference in voting behavior between those who owned real estate and those who owned personal property by portraying the predominantly real estate-oriented individuals as traditionalists who resented the new changes occurring in the community.[39]

Using the Beverly tax valuation records, it is possible to estimate the total taxable wealth of individuals and to subdivide it into personal property and real estate.[40] The total taxable wealth of the individual was subdivided according to the levels of wealth used by Katz and then each of these subcategories was further subdivided by whether the majority of wealth consisted of real estate holdings.[41]

Overall the MCA results confirm Katz's findings. Generally, there is a direct relationship between the taxable wealth of the voter and the probability that he supported the high school—the more wealth an individual possessed, the more likely he was to vote for the high school. Those most likely to oppose the high school, however, were not the least wealthy, as Katz suggested, but those who possessed between $1,000 and $5,000 worth of goods—most of it in real estate. In addition, voters who had most of their wealth in real estate rather than personal property were more likely to oppose the high school. Furthermore, as Katz suggested, the amount and type of wealth is the third best predictor of voting behavior on the high school. Thus, for whatever reasons, those in Beverly who were most likely to pay for the high school through increased taxes were also its strongest supporters—although again the relationship was by no means perfect since three out of every ten individuals whose total personal and real estate property was valued at more than $5,000 opposed the high school.[42]

One of the most interesting variables in this analysis is the occupation of the voter. Katz concluded that occupation was one of the three best predictors of a voter's position on the high school. In order to explore this variable in detail, the occupations of the voters were subdivided into eight categories—taking into account both conceptual considerations as well as the number of individuals in each category. Based upon Katz's work, it was expected that voters in the occupations of merchant, manufacturer, professional and white collar worker, and gentleman and those without any occupations would be more apt to support the Beverly High School than the shoemakers, fishermen, and mariners, and farmers who would be less likely to view that institution as a necessary or desirable goal for their children.[43]

The results, after controlling for the effects of the other variables, generally confirm the initial hypothesis: voters who were merchants, manufacturers, professional and white collar workers, and gentlemen and those without any occupation were more likely to support the high school. Nevertheless, as Katz observed, it is also important to note that the vote from these individual groups was often nearly evenly split on the question of the high school. For example, although much has been made of the role of manufacturers as promoters of educational reforms, half of them voted against the high school—a fact which is not altered by controlling for the other factors.[44] Whether these particular occupational groups supported the high school because of a hope that their own children would attend, a wish to upgrade the quality of education in Beverly, or an unwillingness to defy the state law in, what seemed to many, a hopeless case, cannot be ascertained from the statistical evidence. One suspects that aspects of all three motivations were operating at once with the indictment most certainly a part of the decision making since the majority of Beverly citizens did not endorse the high school until after the indictment was brought against the town.

The voting behavior of the farmers is more difficult to understand. Katz's interpretation of their opposition to the high school is confusing and misleading. When arguing that the working class opposed the high school while the upper and middle classes supported it, Katz classifies the farmers in Beverly as working class;[45] when he tries to demonstrate that only middle class parents sent their children to the Chelsea and Somerville public high schools, he categorizes farmers as middle class.[46] Thus, by assigning two different class designations to farmers, Katz seemingly strengthens his argument that the public high schools were created for the exclusive benefit of the upper and middle classes despite the opposition from the working class.

A simple cross-tabulation shows that 73.0 percent of the farmers voting on the high school issue opposed its establishment. This would seem, without further scrutiny, to suggest firm opposition on their part. After controlling for the other factors, however, the percentage of voting farmers opposed to the high school drops considerably. This suggests that it was not just their occupation that promoted farmers' hostility to the high school but some other characteristics, such as where they lived.[47]

The two occupational subgroups which continued to be the most hostile to the high school even after controlling for the other variables are the shoemakers and the fishermen and mariners. More than 70 percent of the voters in these occupations opposed the high school, and controlling for their other socioeconomic and geographic characteristics only partly reduced that opposition. Katz argues that workers saw little need for or benefit from the high school as far as their children were concerned, and so voted against it, while those in the higher socioeconomic groups did see and want these benefits for their children and therefore voted accordingly.[48] It would seem that the facts support the theory, but it must be noted that 25 to 30 percent of these workers did vote for the high school. In view of the fact that a good-sized segment of the working class voters supported the establishment of the high school and, as noted earlier, a significant portion of voting merchants and manufacturers were against it, the delineation of workers and merchants and manufacturers into two opposing camps, a disposition of forces for which Katz argues long and hard, seems less warranted. Furthermore, Katz sees in the vote of the shoemakers against the high school a protest against industrial development in Beverly. We would expect then that the fishermen and mariner occupational subgroup, being more immune to the kind of disruption that the shoemakers would suffer (as the result of industrial development and the 1860 shoemakers' strike), would be less likely to protest and therefore would cast a lower percentage of negative votes on the high school issue than the shoemakers. The fishermen and mariners, however, did not do that. The MCA shows that after controlling for the other variables among those voting, the fishermen and mariners were even more opposed to establishing a high school than were the shoemakers.[49] Finally, contrary to the conclusions reached by Katz, occupation is not a very good predictor of voting behavior. While differences in voting behavior by the various occupational subcategories exist and persist after controlling for the other factors, the variable itself does not have the explanatory power that Katz suggests—it is only the eighth best predictor of a voter's opinion on the high school among the nine independent variables used in the MCA.

Another event, the New England shoemakers strike, coincided with the 1860 abolition of the Beverly High School. This strike plays an important role in Katz's interpretation of the vote on the high school because he sees in it both a reflection of the deep social and economic tensions within Beverly as it became industrialized and a mechanism by which workers expressed their discontent with the manufacturers and merchants. As he put it:

> The abolition of Beverly high school occurred amidst the greatest social crisis in the history of the town. In the same week that they voted four to one to abolish the high school, the shoemakers of Beverly, the dominant occupational group in town, went on strike and so did thousands of other shoemakers in Essex County. The walkout by Essex County shoemakers in 1860 was the largest strike in the United States before the Civil War.[50]

Katz was unable to find any direct evidence of a link between the strike in Beverly and the outcome of the vote on the Beverly High School. Nevertheless he attempted to establish one. He draws upon indirect evidence and relies upon reports of the strike activities in Lynn to make inferences about the attitude of workers in Beverly.[51] The Beverly workers voted, according to Katz, against the high school because they were rebelling against the wealthy manufacturing and commercial leaders of the community.

> At the time of the high school vote the shoemakers in particular were hostile to the representatives of the manufacturing and commercial interests, who had lowered wages. Yet the tradition of machine breaking and direct physical assault, prominent in other countries, did not spread to America in this period. In voting to abolish the high school, a favorite innovation of their antagonists, the shoemakers had an opportunity to vent their anger in a perfectly legal way.[52]

In Katz's portrayal of the shoe strike, the shoe workers in Beverly readily joined the rest of their New England counterparts in revolting against the increasing mechanization of their trade and protesting the resultant loss of wages and status. He fails to note, however, that the Beverly shoe workers were slow in joining the strike. The somewhat delayed onset of the Beverly strike raises questions about just how extensive and deep tensions were in that community early in 1860.

The Lynn shoe workers began their strike on Washington's birthday (February 22) and were soon joined by strikes in many other communities.[53] By the end of February, it is estimated that Mechanics' Associations had been organized in at least twenty-five towns, and close to 20,000 workers were on strike.[54] Despite the large number of shoe workers in Beverly and the social and economic hardships that they may have been experiencing, they were slow to strike. Throughout the latter part of February, when workers in other communities had already joined the strike, the shoe workers of Beverly were awaiting further developments.[55] Finally, on March 2, 1860, several hundred Beverly shoe workers assembled at the first public meeting in Beverly dealing with the strike, debated the merits of it (with most of them in favor of the strike), but postponed action for another week in order to canvass all of the shoe workers in the community.[56] A week later the workers reconvened and voted to strike on March 13; it would then be almost three weeks since the initial Lynn shoe strike and many days after workers in most other communities had already joined the strike.[57]

Once the Beverly shoe workers did strike, they were very active and united. Indeed, as one Salem newspaper observed:

> The Beverly strikers, with banners and music, passed our office on their way to Lynn. They numbered some three hundred, and

were said to be the largest delegation from abroad. They were accompanied by the Beverly Band, reorganized for the occasion under the lead of Mr. Benj. R. Foster and the whole made a fine appearance.[58]

This enthusiastic participation by the Beverly shoemakers confirms that they were committed to the strike issue, but whether that also confirms a high level of social tension, interclass animosity and worker-manager alienation, especially considering the deliberate and reasoned steps they took in joining the strike is not equally clear.

There are additional reasons to suggest that the Beverly strikers may have been less hostile to local manufacturers and merchants than stated by Katz. Many of the shoe manufacturers, John Knowlton, Francis E. Porter, and John H. Young, for example, openly supported the strikers. Other businessmen in the community also offered considerable support. When the strike procession stopped in front of J. and J. V. Porter's shop, the strikers were presented with two banners—"We Strike for Liberty—Our Cause is Just" and "Beverly-United Efforts Brings Sure Success".[59] Indeed, rather than exhibiting signs of hostility toward local manufacturers and merchants, the shoe workers in Beverly frequently called upon them to address the strikers and cheered when the speaker expressed sympathy for the strike.

Neither can it be shown that the strike polarized the community as much as Katz's study implies. The shoe strike in Lynn did divide that community. The mayor of Lynn called in the militia and mobilized police from surrounding communities, thus destroying whatever unity had previously existed in Lynn.[60] The reaction to the strike by officials in Beverly was very different. The town officials did not try to oppose the strike or to mobilize the police or militia. Instead, the town meeting voted the strikers the use of the town hall for their assemblies. In addition, clergymen like Kimball sympathized with the strike and encouraged the workers to obtain a fair compensation for their labor while also cautioning them to maintain kind feelings toward their employers.[61] Furthermore, while the newspapers in many other communities opposed the strike, the Beverly *Citizen* expressed considerable sympathy for the plight of the strikers and support for their rights and called for a national organization of shoemakers since it appeared at that time that most manufacturers would not agree to the higher wages and prices:

> The efforts of the shoemakers, now in progress, should elect the sympathy of all our citizens who are interested in the welfare of our town. A large part of our population are engaged in the business connected with the manufacture of boots and shoes, and their com-

pensation for some time past has been entirely for their support. We believe that the Bosses in this town are men of integrity and generally disposed to pay a fair price to the Jours for this work. But so many have gone into the business that it has been overdone, and more shoes and boots has [*sic*] been manufactured than the demand required. Another reason which has operated against the business is that many of the shoes manufactured has [*sic*] been of an inferior quality, they having been made by persons who never learned the trade. The strikers have prepared and adopted a bill of prices which they require their employers to agree to. This will not be assented to from what we learn from them—A better plan would be for our Shoemakers to form a National and State Alliance, with subordinate associations in every town and City interested in this business with a constitution for their government, to be signed by all engaged in the business and also to adopt an apprentice system. There is much intelligence among this class of citizens and they are capable if they will act in harmony of obtaining all they require by such an association without the assent of their employers to the bill of wages.[62]

According to Katz, the strikers' vote against the high school was at least in part an act of rebellion against the supporters of the high school and yet some of the staunchest advocates of the Beverly High School were welcomed at the meetings of the strikers. Frederick Choate, a wealthy lawyer and investor who was one of the most visible and active spokesmen for the high school, was called upon at least twice to address the strikers and "spoke eloquently in aid of the cause and pledged to it his full share of aid and comfort."[63]

It is also important to not exaggerate the unanimity of worker opposition to the high school among the leaders of the strike. Among the thirteen leaders of the Beverly shoe strikers identified in the newspapers, only four of them voted against the high school while one supported it.[64] Perhaps the most significant fact is that almost two-thirds of the strike activists either were not present at the meeting to abolish the high school or chose not to vote on that issue. In other words, while most shoe workers recorded at the March meeting voted to abolish the high school, there is little evidence to suggest that this became an important implicit or explicit part of the strike agenda or activities in Beverly.

Thus, while there are occupational differences between those who supported and those who opposed the high school, the differences are not as clearcut nor as important as suggested by Katz's interpretation which emphasizes class tensions within the community as one of the chief motivations for those who succeeded in abolishing the high school. Because the strike undoubtedly exacerbated social and economic divisions within the community, it is perhaps even more remarkable that so much public sympathy was directed toward the shoemakers in Beverly by some of the more prominent and wealthy town leaders—especially remarkable when compared to the experiences of strikers in cities such as Lynn. Rather than see the defeat of the high school mainly as an indication of class hostility stimulated by the shoe strike, one can better account for much of the intensity of the opposition to this facility by focusing on the anger the citizens felt toward having a very expensive and seemingly unnecessary institution forced upon them at a time when the adverse economic effects of the Panic of 1857, which were especially hard on the shoemakers and fishermen, lead many individuals to question the wisdom of any increases in town expenditures.

The vote on the Beverly High School was in the final analysis a local political decision made at the town meeting. Katz however dismisses political considerations in his analysis of the behavior of the voters. Since Wyatt C. Boyden, a Whig, and Robert Rantoul, Sr., a Democrat, cooperated on school affairs, he concluded "that on the local level partisan politics was simply irrelevant, in this period, to education."[65] But since Katz's evidence on local politics is limited to this single statement, it seemed necessary to pursue this issue further.

A previous study of Massachusetts educational politics had found that in the 1840s, while both Whigs and Democrats supported public education at the local level, they divided along party lines in the legislature over the need for a State Board of Education under Horace Mann.[66] To ascertain whether differences between voters who could be identified as former Whigs or Democrats affected the vote on the high school in 1860, the previous political affiliation for 23 of the voters was determined from the local newspaper or lists of those running for office. Naturally, the voters identified in this manner were not typical of Whigs and Democrats in general since, as newsmakers or candidates, they were the more politically active and successful individuals in those parties. Nevertheless, the results are interesting—only 47 percent of those who were former Whigs voted against the high school whereas 67 percent of those who were early Democrats opposed it. After controlling for the effects of the other factors, the difference between the two remained, but overall this variable was not particularly useful as a predictor; it was only the sixth best predictor—perhaps because of the lack of information on former political affiliation for most of the voters.[67]

To see whether political affiliation in 1860 was related to a voter's decision on the high school issue, party affiliation was obtained for 43 of the voters (most of them Republicans). Again, the information on party affiliation was for the most active and successful members of each party rather than the rank-and-file members since the data were obtained from elections and lists of party functionaries in the local newspaper.[68]

Voters who could be identified as Republican or Democratic party members were more supportive of the high school than were voters who could not be linked to a particular political party. After controlling for the effects of the other variables, however, Democratic voters were found to be more opposed to continuing the high school than their Republican counterparts. Overall, the party affiliation variable was the fifth best predictor of voting behavior. Thus, although the high school did not become a partisan issue in Beverly, the Republican-oriented Beverly *Citizen* strongly endorsed it and Republican Party members were more apt to support it than either Democrats or those not identified with either party.

Factors beyond partisan influences must also be considered in the examination of how local political concerns affected the outcome of the vote on the high school. The Beverly town meeting of 1860 was significant not only because of the abolition of the high school, but also because a caucus of citizens had met the week before and nominated a single set of candidates for the most important municipal posts. The candidates on the slate, known as the Citizen's Ticket, were organized by office to be filled and endorsed by the pro-high school Beverly *Citizen*.[69] There were other candidates for at least some of these offices at the town meeting, but there is no evidence of another organized slate. Interestingly, almost all of the individuals on the Citizen's Ticket were supporters of the high school and ministers were nominated for three of the four three-year positions on the Beverly School Board.[70] If the shoemakers and their allies were as angry at the community leaders as is suggested by Katz, surely they would balk at reelecting many of the same town officials who had established the high school two years earlier.[71] Yet, despite whatever tensions there may have been within the community, 38 of the 41 individuals recommended by the Citizen's Ticket were elected.[72]

The results of the election at the 1860 town meeting do not suggest any wholesale dissatisfaction with the political leadership of the community even though most of these leaders supported the new high school. Indeed, one of the individuals on the Citizen's Ticket later shown to be against the high school was replaced by someone who supported the high school. In another contest, the new Unitarian minister, a likely supporter of the high school, was elected in place of the Citizen's Ticket candidate, a nonminister.[73] Thus, while many of the citizens of Beverly were clearly upset and bitter over the establishment of the high school, they did not direct that anger against the local town leaders or the Citizen's Ticket.

Since the town officials elected from the Citizen's Ticket in 1860 were so overwhelmingly in favor of the high school, it seemed reasonable to explore further whether voters who were or had been town officials were more likely to support the high school. In order to construct an index of municipal office holding in Beverly, the town meeting records from 1854 to 1860 were used to create a file of the offices held by each individual during those years. In any given year, approximately 100 town offices had to be filled. Altogether, 698 town offices were filled between 1854 and 1860 by 324 different individuals.[74] Since the office of selectman was considerably more important than that of fence viewer, each office was weighted to reflect its relative status and importance. Thus, selectman was deemed to be twice as prestigious as member of the school committee and six times as important as fence viewer.[75]

The independent variable on town office holding was divided into seven subcategories based upon the number and weight of offices held during the period 1854–60. The relationship between the vote on the high school and office holding shows that the higher the index of office holding, the more likely one was to support the high school. Indeed, the index of town office holding is the second best predictor of a voter's position on the high school.[76]

Interpretations of the findings from the MCA on this variable are not clearcut. One might argue, for instance, that the voters who were more prominent and active leaders of the community supported the high school because they were most aware of and concerned about the social tensions within Beverly and saw the high school as a means of reducing those conflicts. Yet an analysis of the votes on the high school by the elected police officials, who might have been particularly concerned about law and order, indicates that they were less apt to support the high school than voters who were education and welfare officials, town meeting moderators, or town clerks and selectmen, and only slightly more supportive than voters who were town financial officers.

An alternate interpretation might stress the reluctance of the more experienced municipal officials to abolish the high school since it would involve openly defying state law and incur a heavy financial penalty for noncompliance. In addition, some current and former town officials, especially those on the school committee and the board of public library trustees, had been among the staunchest supporters of the high school all along and were probably quite willing to use the threat of the indictment against the town to establish this institution, despite the angry opposition from the town meeting. Thus, while the town political leadership was by no means united on behalf of continuing the high school or in agreement on the reasons for saving it, the voting leaders were much more likely to support it than voters who had not been elected to any town offices or those who held only the least important posts.

The final variable to be considered from this MCA is the school district in which the voter lived. Due to the small number of voters from the smaller districts, it was expedient to combine Bald Hill, East Farms, and West Farms into one category and Bass River, Dodge's Row, and Washington into another. The Cove, the Grammar, and the South districts were large enough to maintain as separate categories.

The school district in which the voter lived was by far the single best predictor of a voter's position on the high school—when taken by itself or when included in the MCA with the eight other independent variables. Voters in the two most populous districts, Grammar and South, were almost evenly split on the high school while those in the other three areas were overwhelmingly opposed to the high school. Especially hostile were voters from the outlying areas of Cove and Bald Hill, East Farms, and West Farms region.[77]

The hostility to the high school of voters from the smaller, outlying school districts is not surprising in view of the earlier discussions of the sectional tensions among the school districts in that community. What is surprising is that Katz, using exactly the same set of data, did not even include sectional differences as one of his three major predictors of voting behavior on the high school.[78] Even more puzzling is why Katz singled out sectional differences as the cause of communal division over the high school in Groton, but rejected the same explanation for the controversy over the Beverly High School.[79]

Although the geographic division on the vote for the high school in Beverly reflected to some degree disagreements over where it should be located, location of the high school was not a major determinant of voting behavior. Otherwise, the Bald Hill, East Farms, and West Farms voters would have supported the high school in large numbers since at the time the high school was located in the West Farms district and the citizens at the town meeting had again rejected efforts to move it elsewhere. Instead, the nearly unanimous opposition to the high school by votes from the outlying districts more likely reflected their conviction that the tax dollars could be better spent on improving common schools in these areas rather than on financing an expensive and underutilized public high school as well as the fear that this was but the first step toward the centralization and consolidation of education in the community.

It is also very interesting to note how contemporaries viewed the clash over the public high school. In the late 1880s when Frederick A. Ober wrote a short history of Beverly, he explained the fight over the establishment of the high school very much along the lines presented in this analysis:

> The High School was not established until after a conflict of several years, the opposition being not so much against the establishment of the school itself as from fear that the money devoted to its support would be proportionately taken from the various districts schools, all of them being popular local institutions, and each with its special neighborhood attractions.
>
> The town had become large enough to be liable in law to support a High School, and some of its friends got so far out of patience in waiting for the town to establish it that they had it indicted. This but intensified the opposition, which was then a decided majority, and they at first attempted to defend the town; but eventually yielded, though the school was at first established at the West Farms, at some distance from the centre of population.[80]

Subsequent events in Beverly shed some additional light on the matter. The town was again indicted for failure to maintain a public high school and came to trial in February 1861 before the Superior Court in Salem. The case was then sent to the State Supreme Court in Boston, which was expected to deal with the issue of constitutionality of the state law as well as the particular procedures involved in the indictment.[81]

In anticipation of the March 1861 town meeting, the Beverly *Citizen* again encouraged voters to reestablish the high school. Letters to the editor sang the praises of a public high school while simultaneously warning of the likely "expense of a fine of thousands of dollars" if the town ignored the indictment.[82] Some citizens feared another tumultuous town meeting. Indeed, one writer advised that the proposed meeting time be changed to the early afternoon so that ladies could sit in the gallery in order to "hold in check the passions of the sterner sex."[83]

At the town meeting in March 1861, a petition of Henry E. Woodberry and others for reestablishing the high school passed after some debate. Then a special committee of one person from each school district and an additional one from each of Grammar, South, Cove, and Washington were chosen to select the most convenient location for the high school.[84] In contrast to the hostility and bitterness prevalent at the March 1860 town meeting, the Beverly *Citizen* characterized this session as peaceful:

> The meeting was unusually harmonious and although several matters elicited considerable earnest discussion, yet the town and temper of the meeting was such throughout as to be evident to all present that the 'era of good feeling' had arrived.[85]

In other words, the rancor and bitterness over the Beverly High School present at the March 1860 meeting had subsided to a large degree only one year later. Perhaps the citizens had sufficiently vented their anger and frustration against the minority who had imposed the high school upon them. Or maybe they had resigned themselves to the fact that nothing could be done since Beverly was about to lose in the State Supreme Court. Or, perhaps, the impending likelihood of a civil war between the North and the South made their local, sectional disagreements over the high school seem somewhat less important. In any case, Katz leaves a very misleading impression about the extent and depth of antagonisms within Beverly by not revealing that the high school was reestablished the next year under much more harmonious conditions.

With the reestablishment of the high school, the indictment against the town was discontinued.[86] The special committee agreed upon the Odd Fellows Hall as a temporary but more convenient location for the high school under the direction of Joseph Hale Abbott.[87] The greater geographic accessibility of the high school to students as well as its apparent permanency led to a significantly larger enrollment—fifty-three of the sixty-four who applied for admission in 1861 were accepted.[88] Although the town continued to be divided over educational issues such as the consolidation of school districts and the centralization of control of public education, the Beverly High School became a permanent and accepted part of public schooling in that community.[89]

This interpretation of the abolition in March 1860 of the Beverly High School draws heavily upon the pioneering analysis by Katz, but departs from it significantly on several key points. Katz argues that the vote is a reflection of opinion about the high school; it is more properly seen as a vote on whether to comply with the state law which required a public high school for towns the size of Beverly. This is an important distinction because the vote by the citizens of Beverly to establish a public high school was not perceived by the town as an act of educational policy or as filling an educational need. It was only when they were faced with an indictment against the town that the citizens voted for a public high school —and even then by a very close margin. As a result, the analysis of the vote to abolish the high school exposes not only the limited extent of individual voter support for such an institution, but also the reluctance of many citizens to do something blatantly illegal—especially when threatened with a sizable monetary penalty for failure to comply with the state law.

This investigation differs from that of Katz in its use of a larger number of factors to explain the event and its use of more sophisticated statistical procedures as well as its attempt to incorporate a great many more findings from traditional historical sources (letters, newspapers, committee reports, sermons, contemporary histories, etc.). These improved techniques have produced results that are very different from those of Katz. The most striking finding is that the two strongest predictive variables in this analysis, location of the voter's residence and the extent of their town office holding, do not figure significantly in Katz's study. In addition, while the general predictive pattern ascertained by Katz for two of his most important variables, children in the household and occupation, continue to persist in this analysis, the relative strength of these variables as predictors of the outcome of the high school vote are considerably less than he suggested. Indeed, the three best predictors in the present analysis (geographic location, town office holding, and wealth) explain 29.4 percent of the total variance of the vote, while the three best predictors in Katz's study (occupation, wealth, and children in household) account for only 9.6 percent.[90] Furthermore, though Katz was correct in pointing to the divisions within the community to account for the disagreements over the high school, he exaggerated the extent of class conflict and seriously underestimated the importance of sectional divisions within the community and the anger felt by many voters toward the imposition of an expensive and seemingly unnecessary institution by a determined minority using the threat of a court indictment against the town.

Thus, although the voters of Beverly rejected the public high school on March 14, 1860, the causes of their action are much more complex than suggested by Katz. It was not a rejection of popular education; the town steadily increased its support for common schools throughout this period. The social and political elites of the community did not succeed in building the high school for their own benefits; the majority of Beverly citizens successfully opposed it several times before the indictment. Instead, a small but effective group of education promoters, using the state law which required towns to build high schools, forced the taxpayers of Beverly to build a public high school. Although they finally succeeded, success was short-lived. The bitterness the struggle had engendered as well as the continuing reluctance of Beverly citizens to fund an expensive and relatively underutilized high school led to its abolition on March 14, 1860. Under further pressure from court proceedings and the efforts of the education promoters the town once again reestablished the high school in March 1861. While the struggle over the Beverly High School does not reveal the type and depth of class tensions suggested by Katz, it does point to the complex process by which towns expand their public school offerings and to the strong disagreements within communities on how to allocate scarce educational funds between common schools and high schools.

5 / Conclusion

THE battle over the Beverly High School in and of itself is not particularly important to the overall development of education in antebellum Massachusetts. Indeed, at that time the controversy was scarcely noticed by contemporaries outside of the town of Beverly. Yet the issues raised by this case study as well as the light shed by the unusual records left from that dispute provide us with some important insights into the nature of antebellum educational reform in New England.

Michael Katz and other revisionists have relied heavily upon the fight over the Beverly High School to demonstrate the efforts of capitalists to impose educational reforms upon unwilling workers. Reacting to the social tensions created by the growing industrialization of Beverly in the 1850s, a small group of the leading capitalists in that community supposedly banded together to establish a public high school not only to provide educational opportunities for their own children, but also to help restore the harmony in the community which was being eroded by the economic transformation of the town.[1]

The present reanalysis of the establishment of the Beverly High School raises serious questions about that interpretation—both in terms of Katz's depiction of the timing and of his reasons for the creation of that institution. Although the high school was not created until 1858, there were efforts to establish it in the early 1840s. Therefore, any attempt to describe the origins of the movement for a public high school in Beverly must take into consideration the socioeconomic conditions in that community at least ten years earlier than the time period emphasized in Katz's study. Since Beverly in the 1840s was not experiencing the amount of economic dislocation that Katz attributed to it in the 1850s, it is more useful to see the origins of the high school in a longer time frame and from the broader perspective of educational developments statewide in Massachusetts rather than to focus mainly on changing conditions within that one community during only part of the period of change.[2]

The citizens in Beverly who championed the high school were influenced to a large degree by similar efforts elsewhere in the Commonwealth. The steady growth in the number of public high schools in the 1830s and 1840s in Massachusetts communities stimulated other cities and towns such as Beverly to attempt to establish high schools—especially since these institutions were advocated and publicized by prominent educational reformers such as Horace Mann.

Particularly important in this process of the diffusion of public high schools throughout the Commonwealth was the enactment and gradual enforcement of legislation requiring such institutions. Many educational historians have underestimated the importance of changes in the law in the development of public education—perhaps because they focused on cases involving flagrant violation of the public school laws regarding compulsory school attendance or truancy and therefore assumed that the statutes were meaningless in practice. Yet the way in which the proponents of the Beverly High School utilized the state law to their advantage at the local level suggests that we need to reconsider the entire relationship between the law and educational change in antebellum America.

The citizens of Massachusetts were generally unwilling to accept the imposition of major changes in local educational institutions or expenditures by the state. Indeed, much of the opposition to the establishment of even a seemingly powerless secretary of the Massachusetts Board of Education in 1837 was due to the fears that the office might someday be used to interfere in what many considered to be a strictly local matter.[3] Although Horace Mann and some of his supporters undoubtedly were eager to expand the power of the state to influence educational reforms at the local level, they were restrained from further efforts by the near demise of the position of the secretary of the Massachusetts Board of Education in the early 1840s.[4]

Under these circumstances, it would have been very difficult and politically foolish for someone like Horace Mann or his immediate successors to initiate legal proceedings against communities which failed to comply with the state statutes requiring each community to establish a public high school. Such action might have simply solidified opposition to public high schools by uniting citizens against what many would have perceived as an unwarranted and dangerous intrusion of the state into local matters. Similarly, although the secretaries of the Massachusetts

Board of Education could have threatened to withhold a community's portion of the state school fund, these allocations were small and the secretaries were unwilling to risk the political costs of such action.[5] Therefore, it is not at all surprising that many Masschusetts communities, especially in the 1830s and 1840s, openly ignored the state laws requiring them to maintain a public high school—a position made easier whenever those laws were changed, as was frequently done, to provide exceptions to their initial requirements.

But if outsiders such as Horace Mann did not feel it prudent to indict communities such as Beverly for failure to establish a public high school, it does not mean that the state laws had no effect whatsoever. Instead, we need to recognize that individuals who wanted to establish a public high school could use the threat of the penalty for noncompliance with the state law to lend muscle to their own local efforts. As we have noted earlier, school committees in other Massachusetts communities frequently cited the state statutes to persuade their fellow townspeople of the need for establishing a public high school. Thus, although the idea of state interference in local educational matters by an authority such as the secretary of the Massachusetts Board of Education was particularly offensive to many, the same interference may have appeared less threatening coming from a local group.

Indeed, this is exactly what occurred in Beverly. A small but persistent group of local educational reformers pushed for a public high school throughout the 1840s and 1850s. They initially restricted themselves to persuasion via arguments such as that public high schools were a sound educational policy, increased the stature of the town, and enhanced equality of opportunity. Their continued failure to convince the community to establish a high school, however, led to the decision in the mid-1850s to invoke the state law. Fearing a substantial fine for failing to maintain a public high school, the town meeting in 1857 reluctantly and by a narrow margin voted to establish it—but only after alienating a majority of voters who then retaliated, first by placing the high school in an inaccessible location and then by abolishing it altogether.

Perhaps what we see in pre-Civil War Beverly is the often painful transition in the attitudes of citizens toward the intrusion of the state into hitherto local affairs such as public education. Some Beverly citizens were unwilling to relinquish control of their local school districts to the town school committee, and many were even less willing to acknowledge the state's right to determine how education should be structured and run in their community—even if denying the state's role meant ignoring state laws. Although the indictment against the town was initiated from within the community, the majority of Beverly voters in the late 1850s still deeply resented this attempt by a minority to overide the wishes of the majority—especially when it resulted in the imposition of such an expensive and seemingly unnecessary institution as the high school.

By the late nineteenth and early twentieth centuries, however, the role of the state in determining the nature and functioning of local education had expanded considerably. Using the state school fund as leverage, the Massachusetts Board of Education increasingly was willing and able to impose its ideas upon the local communities. Although local communities continued to resist intrusions by the state, most citizens gradually accepted or became accustomed to the growing influence of the state in public education.[6]

In the 1850s Beverly citizens were caught in a difficult transition period and they vigorously protested against the meddling of the state in their local educational affairs. But their rebellion did not last long, and the townspeople finally acquiesced in the reestablishment of the high school. Opponents of the high school, however, harbored a bitterness toward those local educational reformers who they felt had betrayed them as well as the principle of majority rule. They also were increasingly aware of the power of the state to influence or sometimes even dictate the nature of educational developments at the local level. Perhaps such events helped to pave the way for the further centralization of district education into the hands of the town school committees as local educational reformers learned to use state power to overcome their own political weakness at home.[7]

If the movement for a public high school in Beverly was influenced by events outside that community, it was also dependent upon the efforts of individuals within it. While the revisionists have emphasized the role of capitalists, especially manufacturers, in providing the leadership and support for antebellum Massachusetts reforms, they have almost totally ignored the role of the Protestant clergy.[8] Yet Beverly ministers were the most active on behalf of public education and were the largest and most active group on the school committees to fight for a public high school.

Except in the work of a few educational historians, the role of the clergy in antebellum education has been slighted.[9] Similarly, while some students of American Protestantism have pointed to the involvement of the clergy in educational reforms, others, especially those who have recently analyzed the ministry as a profession, have ignored this involvement.[10] This is very unfortunate since there are indications that the clergy were deeply involved in educational reforms. A study of seventy-four prominent state leaders in education from 1840 to 1890, for instance, found that about one-third of them were ministers and only 18 percent were businessmen.[11]

In Beverly the Protestant ministers dominated the school committee throughout these twenty years of transition both numerically and often intellectually. Despite theological differences, the ministers seemed to agree among themselves upon the importance of and need for educational expansion and reform. In addition, although there was considerable turnover among the ministers (by the mid-nineteenth century the idea of clergymen remaining in the same office for life had long been abandoned), their support for public education did not diminish.[12] In fact, the ministers were so outspoken and insistent upon the establishment of the high school that they were singled out for attack at the 1860 town meeting by the opponents of that institution.[13]

Given this united leadership among the clergy on the issue of educational reform, one might expect that they could have easily persuaded their congregations to support the high school—especially since almost four out of every ten people who voted that day belonged to one of their churches. Yet there were practical limits to the influence of the clergymen on their parishioners. In fact, after controlling for the effects of the other variables, this study found that those who did not belong to any of the churches were actually slightly more likely to support the high school.

The split between the leadership of the clergy and their flocks on the high school issue suggests that we need to reconsider the influence of religion on voting behavior. While religion may have influenced one's partisan leanings, if only by providing channels of easy communication among like-minded individuals, it does not seem to have been very important in determining one's position on educational reform.[14] Therefore, we need to reassess the nature of nineteenth-century voting behavior to take into consideration not only the ethnocultural and socioeconomic characteristics of the voters, but also the different types of political issues that confronted them.

The experiences of the ministers in Beverly also suggest another interesting aspect of mid-nineteenth-century politics. Citizens, at least those in Beverly, had a tendency to automatically elect the Protestant ministers to the school committee, even when they were at odds with the ministers' policy positions. Beverly citizens who voted against the establishment of the high school in 1860 at the very same meeting elected to the four vacant positions on the school committee clergymen who were advocates of that institution. When the town meeting did try to purge the school committee of some of the ministers in the mid-1850s, the newly elected members resigned in protest. This led to the reelection to the committee of many of the clergymen who had been ousted. Thus, the voters in Beverly found themselves handicapped by their long tradition of placing clergymen on the school committee who did not always adequately represent their views. Even more frustrating was their realization that it was no longer possible to restrain the school committee from acting against the interests of most citizens by simply out voting them in the town meetings—the state had suddenly become a powerful ally of the minority interests represented by these clergymen.[15]

The clergymen in Beverly represented the dominant force on the school committee, and they had many allies—especially among the professionals and business leaders. Katz was quite correct to see the important role of wealthy businessmen and investors such as Robert Rantoul, Sr., and Frederick Choate in fostering public education in Beverly in their many years on the school committee.[16] But while Katz appreciated the role of professionals and capitalists in the development of the public schools in that community, he did not provide us with a very balanced picture of their activities or motivations. His portrayal of Rantoul, in particular, is very narrow and one-sided. Rantoul's active involvement in many other reforms such as abolition of capital punishment is ignored so that the reader is not able to see his overall humanitarian orientation.[17] Similarly, while men like Frederick Choate did play a prominent role in educational reforms, they were never as dominant as the revisionists suggest in light of the fact that among those voting over one-third of the merchants, professionals, and white-collar employees opposed the high school as did 50 percent of the manufacturers. Indeed, after controlling for the effects of the other variables, farmers were more supportive of the high school than any of the occupational subgroups mentioned above.

Yet the support from professionals, white-collar workers, manufacturers, and merchants was important because they represented many of the wealthiest individuals in that community who would be expected to pay a large proportion of the cost of any new public high school. Even if most of these individuals were not the active leaders of the educational reform movement, their support of or at least acquiescence in this effort was indispensable. If this group of wealthier residents of Beverly had opposed unanimously the improvement of public education because of the increase in their taxes, it is unlikely that these reforms could have succeeded. Thus, while the revisionists probably exaggerated the direct input of capitalists such as the manufacturers in the promotion of antebellum Massachusetts educational reforms, the indirect support or passive acceptance by these individuals of those changes was crucial.

Katz and other revisionists have stressed that workers in antebellum Massachusetts were opposed to educational reforms. The revisionists do not see the workers demanding or even supporting public schooling; rather their interpretation has education being imposed upon the workers by anxious capitalists who wanted to use it as a means of social control.[18]

Portraying nineteenth-century workers as opposed to education proves to be inaccurate. As several other scholars have persuasively demonstrated, workers in the late 1820s and early 1830s were very much in favor of public education—although they were unrealistic in their expectations of the improvements education could make in their lives.[19] By the 1840s and 1850s worker enthusiasm for education had declined somewhat, but remained quite visible and strong. Although antebellum workers were not often among the leaders of the effort to expand and improve public education, they usually were at least among those who strongly supported education.[20]

In Beverly the impetus for educational expansion and reform did not originate with the workers but came from the clergy and some of the wealthier individuals in that community. There is little reason to suspect, however, that worker groups such as fishermen and shoemakers opposed the general improvement of the public schools. Their opposition to the high school, which was shared by the majority of Beverly voters, whether workers or not, was not an indication of their antagonism to public education in general so much as their desire to reduce taxes and to improve the common schools rather than to invest in higher education.[21]

Although there undoubtedly was some class antagonism in antebellum Beverly, it existed in much smaller measure than is suggested by Katz or other revisionists.[22] The shoemakers' strike in Beverly did not polarize the town simply along class lines. Wealthy lawyers and investors like Frederick Choate supported the strike even though many of them probably realized that its chances of succeeding were quite small.[23] While most workers opposed the high school as unnecessary and too expensive, some of them, including a few of the leaders of the strike, voted for that institution. Whatever bitterness was generated or fueled by the debates over the high school, it was soon dissipated as the town quickly and relatively harmoniously reestablished the high school just twelve months later. Thus, to portray the vote of the workers on the high school issue as an expression of their deep-seated hostility toward the capitalists brought forth by the divisiveness of the shoe strike is at best simplistic and fails to acknowledge the support of workers for public education in antebellum America.

Although in the 1840s and 1850s the town of Beverly was committed to the expansion and improvement of its public schools, it was divided on the way this should be accomplished—this is due in large part to the wide variations in the quality of education provided at different locales within that community. There is a tendency, especially in studies which rely upon aggregate town data, to ignore or minimize the significance of differences within antebellum communities and to focus only on the variations among them.[24] These studies sacrifice an understanding of intracommunity variations in social, religious, and educational characteristics to the apparently broader understanding to be achieved by looking at intercommunity differences. The present study demonstrates that much of the true picture of a community is lost when one area, through the mere happenstance of its population advantages, skews the statistics and yields a falsely drawn summary of that community. This investigation of Beverly, however, suggests that students located in the more densely populated Grammar School district received an education more like that offered in other urban centers such as Lynn or Salem while those living in the East or West Farms School districts experienced an almost totally different type of schooling and one which was closer to that provided in rural communities such as Boxford.[25] Furthermore, this study suggests that much more attention should be paid to the financial limitations upon the expansion of the public schools faced by many communities. A town like Beverly, which was much less wealthy than Salem, experienced greater difficulty in providing comparable public schooling for its children. Similarly, the rural parts of Beverly had still fewer resources than the more populous and affluent center areas.

The plan to establish a high school was a logical extension of the increasing growth and specialization of public schooling in educationally advanced districts such as the Grammar. The high school made much less sense to the citizens in the outlying areas of Beverly who were still struggling, due to the lack of financial resources, to improve and extend their common schools. It is important to understand that many of the education battles in Beverly in the antebellum period were not over the general desirability of public schooling, but over the question of what were the most pressing needs in each locality and who should have the power to make decisions affecting those needs.

In trying to understand the fights over the Beverly High School in the 1840s and 1850s, it is important that we do not project our own values and assumptions into the past without realizing how they have been shaped by very different circumstances. It is to Katz's credit that he did not try to equate support for the high school with an enlightened or progressive outlook. Given the high costs of public high schools, their limited use and the small percentage of students who actually graduated, the great uncertainty about their economic value to the individual or the community, and the continued need for improvements in the common schools, it is easy to understand why so many citizens of the Commonwealth in the antebellum period opposed public high schools. Indeed, if Beverly had not been facing an indictment for noncompliance, I suspect that many of us might have voted against the high school had we been present at the town meeting in 1857 or 1860. Yet thirty or forty years later, after public high schools became more common and societally defined as a necessary part of one's education and career development, we probably would have voted for it.[26] Thus, an interesting and difficult question remains—was it necessary or even desirable to force a reluctant citizenry to establish public high schools which at that time seemed too expensive and unnecessary in order to develop the eventual support for public secondary education and foster a redefinition of what constitutes an adequate education?

This study of public schooling in Beverly also reinforces one of the points raised earlier—that it is essential for analysts of antebellum educational reform to specify more precisely the exact aspect of these developments that they are studying. While the citizens of Beverly steadily shifted the burden and responsibility for educating their children from private to public schools and increased the amount of expenditures on them, at the same time voters opposed a public high school until it was forced upon them. Many of the citizens who voted against the high school may have been just as committed to public schooling as those who supported it, but simply disagreed on the need for or wisdom of a high school to be the particular form for their educational investments.

Educational reform in Beverly was shaped not only by the variations in demographic and socioeconomic characteristics among the local school districts, but also by the general economic and social context in which it occurred. Katz has emphasized the tensions and possible turmoil within the community, especially during the 1850s, as shoemakers in Beverly were transformed from artisans into wage earners.[27] It is also important to note that the great increases in public school expenditures occurred during a period of relative growth and prosperity throughout the Commonwealth so that the proportion of taxable wealth actually spent on schooling in Beverly decreased.[28] The transformation of the Massachusetts economy in general and the Beverly economy in particular not only generated social tensions which education was seen as necessary for alleviating, but also generated the economic prosperity which helped to minimize the burden which increasing educational opportunity would place on the taxpayers.[29] Indeed, while the early efforts to establish a public high school in Beverly were defeated, the town was willing to expend that same amount of additional money on improvements for the common schools. Yet this generous attitude toward public school expansion came to an abrupt end when the economic difficulties triggered by the Panic of 1857 reached the citizens of Beverly.

This reconsideration of the fight over the Beverly High School not only provides insights into the nature and process of educational reform in antebellum America, but it also illustrates the value of analyzing quantitative data to reconstruct the past. While in most settings one could debate forever the relative importance of factors such as class, wealth, or geographic location in explaining the behavior of mid-nineteenth-century voters without reaching a satisfactory conclusion, the unusual availability of the names of the supporters and opponents of the Beverly High School permits the use of statistical techniques which can help to sort out the relative importance of each of the variables.

Part of the disagreement with Katz's findings in his earlier study stems from the use of more sophisticated statistical techniques in this investigation such as multiple classification analysis, but some of the differences reflect the addition of new variables in this analysis such as municipal office holding, political affiliation, and church membership. While not all of these factors are strong predictors of the pattern of voting on the high school, they expand considerably the breadth of this study and place the importance of the other variables such as wealth and occupation in a larger context.

Although this reanalysis grew out of my previous work on the politics of common school reform and the questioning of the use of statistics by Katz in his study, a surprisingly large amount of the revision is the result of a different reconstruction of the events leading to the vote on March 14, 1860. Rather than seeing the more traditional aspects of historical work as quite distinct and separate from the use of quantitative analysis, this case study reaffirms the importance of using both approaches. While statistical analysis can help to ascertain the relative importance of various factors when the appropriate quantifiable data and models are available, it is still essential to place the results within their proper historical sequence and context. Thus, one can often learn as much about an historical event from the reading of the town meeting records or the local newspaper as from analyzing the pattern of voting. Combining both of these analytic strategies permits us to reconstruct the past more accurately than if we had to choose between them.

Having considered the developments in Beverly, Massachusetts, in the twenty years before the Civil War, it is useful to step back and reflect for a moment on the larger issue of the use of quantification in the study of education. At present, the field of American educational history is an exciting and promising area of scholarship—especially in the analysis of antebellum educational development. It has attracted some of the most talented and energetic young scholars and has become closely integrated with other areas such as economic, family, and urban history. Although many controversies and unresolved issues remain, participants are engaged in a healthy dialogue over the conceptual and methodological differences.

The use of social science techniques, especially in the analysis of quantitative data, has played a key role in the evolution of educational history from a minor subspecialty of social history to one of the major components of that field today. Many of the scholars interested in American educational history were trained in other areas such as economic, demographic, or family history and have brought to the history of education the new ideas and techniques of their specialities—especially the analysis of quantitative materials. In turn, these scholars have taken back to their former areas the important findings both conceptual and methodological, of their investigations of educational history. Most of these scholars have acknowledged the strengths and weaknesses of quantitative analysis so that their disagreements are not over the appropriateness of this approach, but over the substantive and methodological differences arising from their research. Most important of all, the willingness to utilize quantitative data and social science techniques of analysis has meant that debates among these scholars have sharpened conceptually and that the issues are often tested empirically. As a result, there is a definite sense of development in this field as scholars react to each other, adjust their hypotheses, and try different approaches to take advantage of new ideas and techniques of analysis.

The one potentially troublesome trend on the horizon is that the tenor of debate about educational history in America has become much more acrimonious as the so-called revisionists are attacked not only for the quality of their analyses, but also for their ideological orientations. Although all work in this field, as in any other, needs constant scrutiny and reexamination, I am not convinced that the questioning, implicit or explicit, of the motives of the participants is fruitful. Rather it would be preferable that the issues be arraigned on substantive and methodological grounds regardless of the orientation of the individuals involved.

Similarly, while I can appreciate the anger and frustration of these revisionist historians about the nature of the recent attacks on their scholarship, a more appropriate and useful response would be to refute the charges leveled against their work or to modify their position to take into consideration any of the valid criticisms from a scholarly perspective. Raising questions about why someone was asked to do a particular review of the field, however, is not likely to advance scholarship any further than the original accusations.

In other words, the recent debate among some educational historians over the ideological motivations of groups of scholars or the political implications of their efforts is likely to be counterproductive in the long run unless it leads to a more scholarly and objective reexamination of the work in this area. If this debate simply degenerates into accusations and counteraccusations, a direction it sometimes appears to be taking, there is little to be gained by anyone. Furthermore, as we are in the process of improving on each other's work, it is important to remember the intellectual debts we owe to those before us—even if we happen to disagree with their earlier interpretations. Thus, while I may differ significantly from Katz in my interpretation of the events in Beverly, I am very appreciative of and dependent upon his pioneering efforts on this issue fifteen years ago.

I am not naively arguing that we ignore the reality that all of us, in varying degrees, are limited by our biases; rather I think we need to be as explicit as possible about our preconceptions and specify as precisely as possible our statements about educational developments in order to clarify our positions, not only for others, but also for ourselves. Then the most important task will be to develop ways of testing these different hypotheses. Although we will never arrive at any ultimate consensus, since honest differences of opinion on scholarly matters are a normal part of the uncertainties of life in the past as well as in the present, we will narrow our areas of disagreement considerably. It is hoped that this reanalysis of the innovative work by Katz on the establishment and abolition of the Beverly High School may serve as a modest illustration of the gradual, but substantive, progress that can be made toward a better understanding of these topics through a dialogue among the participants based upon the employment of social science techniques and the use of quantitative data whenever possible.

Appendix

Notes

Index

Appendix

Table A1.1. Percentage of Whites Ages 0–19 Attending Schools, 1840–60

	1840	1850	1860
New England	81.8	76.2	73.8
Middle Atlantic	49.5	61.9	61.3
South Atlantic	16.2	29.7	31.5
North Central	29.0	51.9	70.3
South Central	13.4	28.4	40.1

Source: Maris A. Vinovskis and Richard M. Bernard, "Beyond Catherine Beecher: Female Education in the Antebellum Period," *Signs* 3, no. 4 (Summer 1978): 856–69.

Table A2.1. Percentage of Persons Ages 0–19 Enrolled in Schools, 1840–60

Year	Massachusetts	Essex County	Salem	Beverly
1840	63.7	50.7	42.4	42.3
1841	64.7	53.2	45.0	50.7
1842	63.6	52.7	47.0	49.8
1843	63.2	54.7	48.9	51.9
1844	63.1	53.7	47.0	50.4
1845	62.2	54.8	49.3	51.6
1846	61.5	53.3	48.4	57.5
1847	62.3	54.7	50.4	58.5
1848	62.7	55.2	47.9	57.7
1849	63.5	55.4	48.0	60.8
1850	62.9	57.5	55.4	63.4
1851	62.4	59.5	56.0	66.2
1852	56.1	59.3	57.2	65.5
1853	60.8	59.2	57.3	65.3
1854	58.5	57.6	59.2	62.2
1855	58.2	55.6	57.3	59.6
1856	59.3	60.2	56.8	58.6
1857	56.9	53.9	57.5	64.5
1858	59.1	55.1	53.0	55.8
1859	57.2	54.2	59.5	54.1
1860	56.8	56.2	54.4	55.4

Source: Calculated from U.S. Censuses of 1840, 1850, and 1860 and Massachusetts Census of 1855; and from the Massachusetts Board of Education, *Annual Reports* for 1839–40 through 1859–60.

Table A2.2. Percentage of Total Annual School Enrollment in Private Schools, 1840–60

Year	Massachusetts	Essex County	Salem	Beverly
1840	12.9	14.4	22.5	17.6
1841	13.5	16.2	24.7	14.9
1842	12.2	14.8	18.7	17.0
1843	11.3	12.8	14.9	15.6
1844	10.7	13.3	12.6	15.1
1845	11.0	12.5	14.3	14.7
1846	9.9	10.8	11.3	14.0
1847	10.6	10.0	10.3	13.5
1848	10.3	11.2	11.9	12.8
1849	10.0	10.0	11.3	12.4
1850	10.6	11.0	18.9	15.6
1851	9.3	11.9	18.8	15.7
1852	9.8	12.5	18.1	15.1
1853	9.8	12.3	19.7	13.0
1854	9.5	12.7	18.3	11.4
1855	9.7	12.7	23.2	8.4
1856	9.9	10.5	22.0	8.5
1857	10.0	11.8	27.6	10.4
1858	9.1	10.4	28.2	.9
1859	9.4	11.7	28.4	4.4
1860	8.0	10.2	18.7	4.5

Source: Calculated from the Massachusetts Board of Education, *Annual Reports* for 1839–40 through 1859–60.

Note: For the years 1840–49, the estimate of the number of public school students who attended private schools only to prolong the public school year has not been included in the total of private school students.

Table A2.3. Average Daily Public and Private Attendance as a Percentage of All Children Ages 0–19, 1840–60

Year	Massachusetts	Essex County	Salem	Beverly
1840	37.1	30.3	27.7	28.4
1841	37.7	32.3	30.0	32.1
1842	36.4	31.3	31.5	31.5
1843	36.1	32.5	34.7	32.6
1844	36.1	32.0	33.4	32.2
1845	36.1	31.9	33.7	32.5
1846	35.6	32.9	39.0	34.0
1847	38.2	35.0	37.7	37.1
1848	38.0	35.2	36.6	34.4
1849	37.5	34.6	33.4	38.1
1850	38.1	36.3	39.4	41.9
1851	37.3	38.5	41.2	42.2
1852	36.8	37.4	41.7	40.7
1853	37.1	37.2	42.1	36.8
1854	35.9	36.6	44.7	37.8
1855	35.9	35.4	43.6	37.0
1856	36.9	36.2	40.2	35.6
1857	35.7	34.8	39.3	42.4
1858	37.1	36.0	38.8	34.8
1859	36.2	35.0	40.5	34.0
1860	36.2	35.6	35.9	33.0

Source: Calculated from U.S. Censuses of 1840, 1850, and 1860 and Massachusetts Census of 1855; and from the Massachusetts Board of Education, *Annual Reports* for 1839–40 through 1859–60.

Table A2.4. Length of Public School Sessions, 1840–60 (in days)

Year	Massachusetts	Essex County	Salem	Beverly
1840	150	175	281	195
1841	158	179	264	194
1842	160	199	264	218
1843	159	177	264	188
1844	163	192	264	191
1845	166	197	264	210
1846	166	195	264	195
1847	168	201	264	215
1848	167	208	264	218
1849	168	215	264	218
1850	162	187	253	217
1851	164	187	253	188
1852	166	198	242	189
1853	166	207	253	211
1854	167	200	253	206
1855	168	206	242	224
1856	168	206	233	207
1857	169	207	241	207
1858	169	202	259	207
1859	172	203	259	203
1860	172	202	253	242

Source: Calculated from the Massachusetts Board of Education, *Annual Reports* for 1839–40 through 1859–60.

Table A2.5. Average Number of Days of Public or Private School Attended per Person under 20 Years of Age, 1840–60

Year	Massachusetts	Essex County	Salem	Beverly
1840	60.6	59.5	87.0	59.1
1841	63.8	65.7	91.1	65.8
1842	62.2	69.2	92.4	70.7
1843	60.0	62.3	99.3	65.0
1844	61.6	67.5	94.6	64.5
1845	62.4	67.2	96.5	71.0
1846	62.5	67.0	108.9	70.2
1847	66.5	74.6	105.2	80.7
1848	65.2	77.8	102.8	77.1
1849	65.2	76.4	94.0	84.5
1850	63.0	68.0	100.4	87.9
1851	61.7	72.1	105.0	77.4
1852	61.4	73.5	102.7	75.9
1853	61.9	76.0	107.5	75.4
1854	60.3	72.7	114.0	75.7
1855	60.6	72.0	107.6	80.7
1856	62.2	73.9	96.6	72.1
1857	60.5	71.1	97.4	85.7
1858	62.9	72.3	101.1	71.9
1859	62.4	70.4	105.5	68.4
1860	62.3	71.3	91.7	78.4

Source: Calculated from U.S. Censuses of 1840, 1850, and 1860 and Massachusetts Census of 1855; and from the Massachusetts Board of Education, *Annual Reports* for 1839–40 through 1859–60.

Table A2.6. School Expenditures per $1,000 of Valuation, 1840–60 (in dollars)

Year	Massachusetts	Essex County	Salem	Beverly
1840	2.85	3.36	2.82	3.84
1841	2.73	3.40	2.72	3.69
1842	2.52	3.00	2.43	3.77
1843	2.24	2.88	2.53	3.48
1844	2.23	2.75	2.33	3.28
1845	2.11	2.59	2.14	3.50
1846	2.07	2.45	2.06	3.30
1847	2.10	2.40	2.00	3.26
1848	2.15	2.46	2.22	2.97
1848	2.17	2.43	2.21	2.46
1850	2.15	2.42	2.10	2.27
1851	2.17	2.52	2.21	2.55
1852	2.05	2.53	2.18	2.43
1853	2.00	2.59	2.26	2.45
1854	2.05	2.73	2.25	2.55
1855	2.17	2.77	2.23	2.56
1856	2.22	2.83	2.43	2.47
1857	2.27	2.85	2.50	2.56
1858	2.28	2.81	2.33	1.99
1859	2.22	2.62	2.33	2.37
1860	2.21	2.59	2.45	2.30

Source: Calculated from Massachusetts Board of Education, *Annual Reports* for 1839–40 through 1859–60.

Table A2.7. Amount of Money Spent for Schools per Person, Age 0–19, 1840–60, in Dollars Adjusted for Cost of Living (1860 = 100)

Year	Massachusetts	Essex County	Salem	Beverly
1840	2.53	2.36	4.36	2.34
1841	2.55	2.48	4.21	2.35
1842	2.69	2.45	4.08	2.69
1843	2.84	2.70	4.71	2.87
1844	2.85	2.65	4.34	2.78
1845	2.78	2.55	3.98	3.06
1846	2.80	2.46	3.83	2.97
1847	2.74	2.31	3.48	2.82
1848	3.03	2.53	4.06	2.77
1849	3.25	2.65	4.21	2.45
1850	3.25	2.63	3.94	2.28
1851	3.43	2.87	4.19	2.70
1852	3.27	2.90	4.06	2.63
1853	3.26	3.03	4.17	2.74
1854	3.13	3.01	3.78	2.71
1855	3.28	3.01	3.61	2.71
1856	3.50	3.20	3.98	2.75
1857	3.55	3.20	3.94	2.86
1858	3.86	3.40	3.87	2.43
1859	3.79	3.20	3.79	2.93
1860	3.85	3.22	3.96	2.93

Source: Calculated from U.S. Censuses of 1840, 1850, and 1860 and Massachusetts Census of 1855; and from the Massachusetts Board of Education, *Annual Reports* for 1839–40 through 1859–60. The cost of living adjustment data are from Paul A. David and Peter Solar, "A Bicentenary Contribution to the History of the Cost of Living in America," *Research in Economic History* 2 (1977), 1–80.

Table A2.8. Amount of Money Spent for Public Schools per Person, Age 0–19, 1840–60, in Dollars Adjusted for Cost of Living (1860 = 100)

Year	Massachusetts	Essex County	Salem	Beverly
1840	1.65	1.30	1.64	1.03
1841	1.66	1.31	1.72	1.03
1842	1.79	1.39	1.89	1.09
1843	1.91	1.65	2.46	1.23
1844	1.95	1.67	2.53	1.16
1845	1.94	1.64	2.38	1.47
1846	2.01	1.64	2.30	1.48
1847	1.95	1.55	2.15	1.37
1848	2.23	1.71	2.47	1.41
1849	2.45	1.88	2.66	1.44
1850	2.44	1.92	2.54	1.40
1851	2.60	2.20	2.79	1.76
1852	2.50	2.26	2.72	1.73
1853	2.57	2.36	2.66	1.95
1854	2.43	2.35	2.54	1.99
1855	2.56	2.48	2.60	2.31
1856	2.73	2.63	2.71	2.35
1857	2.75	2.67	2.59	2.27
1858	2.93	2.84	2.60	2.39
1859	2.99	2.66	2.53	2.76
1860	3.02	2.73	2.61	2.74

Source: See table A2.7.

Table A2.9. Cost per Hundred Days of School Attended, 1840–60, in Dollars Adjusted for Cost of Living (1860 = 100)

Year	Massachusetts	Essex County	Salem	Beverly
1840	4.18	3.96	5.01	3.96
1841	4.00	3.77	4.62	3.57
1842	4.31	3.54	4.42	3.80
1843	4.68	4.34	4.75	4.41
1844	4.62	3.92	4.59	4.32
1845	4.46	3.79	4.13	4.31
1846	4.48	3.67	3.51	4.23
1847	4.12	3.09	3.31	3.50
1848	4.68	3.26	3.95	3.60
1849	5.01	3.46	4.47	2.90
1850	5.15	3.87	3.92	2.60
1851	5.56	3.98	4.00	3.49
1852	5.32	3.95	3.96	3.47
1853	5.27	4.00	3.88	3.64
1854	5.19	4.14	3.32	3.58
1855	5.40	4.18	3.36	3.36
1856	5.62	4.33	4.12	3.82
1857	5.87	4.50	4.04	3.34
1858	6.14	4.70	3.83	3.38
1859	6.08	4.54	3.60	4.29
1860	6.19	4.51	4.32	3.73

Source: See table A2.7.

Table A2.10. Cost per Hundred Days of Public School Attended, 1840–60, in Dollars Adjusted for Cost of Living (1860 = 100)

Year	Massachusetts	Essex County	Salem	Beverly
1840	3.49	3.00	2.83	2.33
1841	3.31	2.82	3.01	2.00
1842	3.60	2.75	2.88	2.00
1843	3.80	3.41	3.19	2.47
1844	3.86	3.26	3.31	2.29
1845	3.77	3.11	3.17	2.60
1846	3.91	2.95	2.49	2.72
1847	3.50	2.49	2.41	2.04
1848	4.02	2.68	2.90	2.24
1849	4.46	2.86	3.44	2.04
1850	4.55	3.25	3.19	1.86
1851	4.80	3.55	3.32	2.73
1852	4.62	3.58	3.31	2.75
1853	4.74	3.60	3.12	3.03
1854	4.58	3.76	2.74	2.97
1855	4.81	4.01	3.20	3.10
1856	5.01	4.05	3.77	3.55
1857	5.17	4.30	3.92	2.93
1858	5.25	4.43	3.63	3.35
1859	5.39	4.34	3.51	4.21
1860	5.36	4.32	3.64	3.64

Source: See table A2.7.

Table A2.11. Cost per Hundred Days of Private School Attended, 1840–60, in Dollars Adjusted for Cost of Living (1860 = 100)

Year	Massachusetts	Essex County	Salem	Beverly
1840	6.65	6.56	9.34	8.82
1841	6.54	6.02	7.35	8.98
1842	6.98	5.74	8.18	10.02
1843	8.97	7.52	10.17	10.86
1844	8.13	6.01	10.04	11.67
1845	7.74	6.26	7.48	10.81
1846	8.46	7.26	9.16	9.45
1847	7.37	6.12	8.45	10.69
1848	8.52	5.84	9.09	9.64
1849	8.12	7.11	9.31	7.34
1850	8.61	7.96	6.75	6.82
1851	11.00	6.72	6.74	7.36
1852	10.52	6.18	6.57	6.99
1853	8.97	6.53	6.77	7.18
1854	9.66	6.40	5.81	8.22
1855	9.64	5.24	3.85	6.52
1856	9.99	6.35	5.13	6.64
1857	10.85	5.84	4.30	7.14
1858	13.15	6.79	4.32	6.84
1859	11.44	5.91	3.79	6.14
1860	14.07	6.03	6.71	5.99

Source: See table A2.7.

Table A2.12. Percentage of Beverly School Committee Members Who Were Ministers, 1841–60

Year	Percent
1841	58.3
1842	58.3
1843	58.3
1844	54.5
1845	50.0
1846	58.3
1847	54.5
1848	58.3
1849	58.3
1850	58.3
1851	36.4
1852	30.0
1853	45.5
1854	54.5
1855	18.2
1856	15.4
1857	30.8
1858	55.6
1859	30.8
1860	41.7

Source: Calculated from the Beverly Town Meeting Records, 1841–60.

Table A3.1. Year First Public High Schools Established in Massachusetts Towns, 1821–65

Year	Number	Year	Number
1821	1	1844	0
1822	0	1845	2
1823	0	1846	2
1824	1	1847	0
1825	0	1848	2
1826	0	1849	11
1827	3	1850	7
1828	1	1851	11
1829	1	1852	12
1830	0	1853	3
1831	2	1854	10
1832	0	1855	7
1833	0	1856	7
1834	0	1857	2
1835	3	1858	4
1836	3	1859	5
1837	6	1860	1
1838	4	1861	0
1839	1	1862	2
1840	0	1863	1
1841	3	1864	7
1842	1	1865	8
1843	1	Total	135

Source: Emit Duncan Grizzell, *Origin and Development of the High School in New England before 1865* (New York: Macmillan, 1923), pp. 94, 132, 146–49.

Notes

INTRODUCTION

1 Although there are some other developments, these two changes have been particularly important. For an overview of some of the recent innovations, see Sol Cohen, "The History of Education in the United States, Historians of Education and Their Discontents," in *Urban Education in the Nineteenth Century: Proceedings of the 1976 Annual Conference of the History of Education Society of Great Britain,* ed. D. A. Reeder (London: Taylor and Francis, 1977), pp. 115–32; Lawrence A. Cremin, *Traditions of American Education* (New York: Basic Books, 1977); Michael B. Katz, "The Origins of Public Education: A Reassessment," *History of Education Quarterly* 16, no. 4 (Winter 1976): 381–407.

2 There is considerable debate over exactly what is meant by the term revisionist—especially since it encompasses such a diverse group of scholars. For the purposes of this study which concentrates on the antebellum period, however, the term is more meaningful—particularly since most of the individuals cited accept Katz's interpretation of the Beverly High School vote. For a discussion of the term, see Diane Ravitch, *The Revisionists Revised: A Critique of the Radical Attack on the Schools* (New York: Basic Books, 1978); Katz, "The Origins of Public Education."

3 Ravitch, *The Revisionists Revised.*

4 Walter Feinberg, Harvey Kantor, Michael Katz, and Paul Violas, *Revisionists Respond to Ravitch* (Washington, D.C.: National Academy of Education, 1980). Ravitch's work has also been strongly criticized by some nonrevisionist historians. Indeed, Tyack even argues that "in her own way she has done what she criticized in her opponents, for she too has politicized history." See David B. Tyack, "Politicizing History," *Reviews in American History* 7, no. 1

(March 1979): 13–17. For a more favorable, though still quite critical, review of Ravitch, see Joseph F. Kett, "On Revisionism," *History of Education Quarterly* 19, no. 2 (September 1979): 229–35.

5 Maris A. Vinovskis, "Trends in Massachusetts Education, 1826–1860," *History of Education Quarterly* 12 (Winter 1972): 501–29; Maris A. Vinovskis, "Horace Mann on the Economic Productivity of Education," *New England Quarterly* 43, no. 4 (December 1970): 550–71.

6 Carl F. Kaestle and Maris A. Vinovskis, *Education and Social Change in Nineteenth-Century Massachusetts* (Cambridge: Cambridge University Press, 1980).

7 Ibid., pp. 208–32.

8 For a thoughtful introduction to the study of the ideology of school reformers, see Carl F. Kaestle, "Presidential Address—Ideology and American Educational History," *History of Education Quarterly* 22, no. 2 (Summer 1982), 123–37.

9 Michael B. Katz, *The Irony of Early School Reform: Educational Innovation in Mid-Nineteenth Century Massachusetts* (Cambridge: Harvard University Press, 1968).

10 Michael W. Sedlack and Timothy Walch, *American Education History: A Guide to Information Sources* (Detroit: Gale Research Company, 1981), p. 22. Henretta praises Katz's study of Beverly as one of the few "new" social histories able to combine both quantitative analysis with the chronological narrative. James A. Henretta, "Social History as Lived and Written," *American Historical Review* 84, no. 5 (December 1979), 1293–1322.

11 David Tyack and Elisabeth Hansot, *Managers of Virtue: Public School Leadership in America, 1820–1980* (New York: Basic Books, 1982), p. 271.

12 Ravitch, *Revisionists Revised*, p. 116.

13 For example, see Samuel Bowles and Herbert Gintis, *Schooling in Capitalist America: Educational Reform and the Contradictions of Economic Life* (New York: Basic Books, 1976), pp. 155–56.

14 Neil Harris, "Review of the Irony of Early School Reform" *Harvard Educational Review* 39 (Spring 1969): 383–89.

15 Diane Ravitch, *The Revisionists Revised*, pp. 116–25. Although Ravitch did not attempt a thorough reanalysis of Katz's work, her hunches about the shortcomings of that volume are quite astute, and many of her criticisms will be sustained, as we shall see, by this investigation—especially her suspicion that Katz underestimated the role of geography.

Similar reservations have been raised in the recent dissertation which looks at the establishment of public high schools in Needham, Massachusetts. Sylvia Olfson Shapiro, "Sources of Inequality: Social Theory, Social History and Educational Policy," unpub. Ph.D. diss. (Harvard University, 1981). While the Shapiro dissertation asks some very perceptive questions and provides useful insights into educational developments in Needham, the conceptual framework is not very precise analytically and the statistics used are rather unsophisticated.

16 Michael B. Katz, "An Apology for American Educational History," *Harvard Educational Review* 69, no. 2 (May 1979): 256–66. Katz makes a series of telling criticisms of Ravitch's book but does not really answer many of her specific questions about his study of Beverly. For example, although Katz points out that he did use geography in his analysis of the high school controversy, he did not consider it to be one of his top three predictors of the vote.

17 Katz, *Irony of Early School Reform.*

18 Kaestle and Vinovskis, *Education and Social Change.*

19 The reader should be aware that the analysis of the Beverly High School controversy constituted only about one-third of the volume by Katz. The other two sections deal with the attack by the American Institution of Instruction on one of its foremost colleagues and the criticisms of the state reform school by some of Massachusetts' leading reformers (*Irony of Early School Reform,* pp. 115–211). This reanalysis is focused only on the issue of the origins and demise of Beverly High School and does not address the other two topics.

20 Alexander James Field, "Economic and Demographic Determinants of Educational Commitment: Massachusetts, 1855," *Journal of Economic History* 39, no. 2 (June 1979): 439–59; Kaestle and Vinovskis, *Education and Social Change.*

21 There are other indications of the need for more in-depth studies of local communities. Katz, for example, found significant educational differences in various sections of Groton (*Irony of Early School Reform,* pp. 62–80). Similarly, the earlier study by Kaestle and myself also pointed to the importance of looking at local communities such as Boxford and Lynn (*Education and Social Change,* pp. 139–85).

22 Katz, *Irony of Early School Reform.*

23 The most detailed discussions of the origins of antebellum Massachusetts public high schools remain those included in books published more than fifty years ago: Alexander James Inglis, *The Rise of the High School in Massachusetts* (New York: Teachers College, 1911); Emit Duncan Grizzell, *Origin and Development of the High School in New England before 1865* (New York: Macmillan, 1923).

24 Katz, *Irony of Early School Reform.*

25 More recent efforts to analyze nineteenth-century public high schools usually have not been concerned with their origin prior to the Civil War. For example, see Edward A. Krug, *The Shaping of the American High School, 1880–1920* (Madison: University of Wisconsin Press, 1964).

26 Katz, *Irony of Early School Reform.*

CHAPTER 1

1 Diane Ravitch, *The Revisionists Revised: A Critique of the Radical Attack on the School* (New York: Basic Books, 1978); Walter Feinberg, Harvey Kantor,

Michael Katz, and Paul Violas, *Revisionists Respond to Ravitch* (Washington, D.C.: National Academy of Education, 1980). For good general introductions to the use of quantification in educational history, see Harvey J. Graff, "The 'New Math': Quantification, the 'New' History, and the History of Education," *Urban Education* 11, no. 4 (January 1977): 403–40; David L. Angus, "The Empirical Mode: Quantitative History," in *Historical Inquiry in Education: As Research Agenda,* ed. John Hardin Best (Washington, D.C.: American Educational Research Association, 1983), pp. 75–93. For a discussion of some of the methodological and conceptual problems in this field, see Maris A. Vinovskis, "Community Studies in Urban Educational History: Some Methodological and Conceptual Observations," in *Schools in Cities: Consensus and Conflict in American Educational History,* eds. Ronald K. Goodenow and Diane Ravitch (New York: Holmes and Meier, 1983), pp. 287–304.

2 Samuel Bowles and Herbert Gintis, *Schooling in Capitalist America: Educational Reform and the Contradictions of Economic Life* (New York: Basic Books, 1976), pp. 178–79.

3 Ibid., p. 154.

4 Kenneth A. Lockridge, *Literacy in Colonial New England: An Inquiry into the Social Context of Literacy in the Early Modern West* (New York: Norton, 1974). For a critique of this interpretation of the literacy of women, see Gerald F. Moran and Maris A. Vinovskis, "The Great Care of Godly Parents: Early Childhood in Puritan New England," in *Child Development in Historical Perspective,* eds. Alice Smuts and John Hagen (forthcoming); Carl F. Kaestle and Maris A. Vinovskis, *Education and Social Change in Nineteenth-Century Massachusetts* (Cambridge: Cambridge University Press, 1980), pp. 9–27. Our analysis of the trends in this earlier period is a revision of the important work of Albert Fishlow, "The American Common School Revival: Fact or Fancy?" in *Industrialization in Two Systems: Essays in Honor of Alexander Gershenkron,* ed. Henry Rosovsky (New York: Wiley, 1966), pp. 40–67.

5 Alexander James Field, "Economic and Demographic Determinants of Educational Commitment: Massachusetts, 1855," *Journal of Economic History* 39, no. 2 (June 1979): 439–59.

6 Ibid., p. 450.

7 On the crisis in rural education, see Kaestle and Vinovskis, *Education and Social Change,* pp. 115–24. Carl Kaestle and Maris A. Vinovskis, "Quantification, Urbanization, and the History of Education: An Analysis of the Determinants of School Attendance in New York State in 1845," *Historical Methods Newsletter* 8, no. 1 (December 1974): 1–9.

8 The analysis of the origins of mass public education by Bowles and Gintis is strange in that they are aware of the great expansion of public education outside the Northeast but then ignore the implications of this important fact for their argument. Their efforts to account for the rise of mass public education in the decades prior to the Civil War outside the Northeast are limited and

their findings are inaccurate. Bowles and Gintis, *Schooling in Capitalist America,* pp. 174–78. For a good critique of their functionalist approach, see David K. Cohen and Bella H. Rosenberg, "Functions and Fantasies: Understanding Schools in Capitalist America," *History of Education Quarterly* 17, no. 2 (Summer 1977): 113–37, as well as the interesting discussions of that paper, including remarks by Bowles and Gintis, ibid., pp. 139–68. Field, unlike Bowles and Gintis, does not try to argue from the example of Massachusetts to the rest of antebellum America. He is unusually careful in delineating the proper limitations of generalizing from his case study of one state to developments elsewhere in all of his writings.

The U.S. Census of 1850 and 1860 requested information on the total number of students from both schools and families. Although the results are similar, they are not identical. In 1840 the number of students was only obtained from the schools.

Census definitions provide the basis for the regions used in this chapter. All states and territories within the census regions were included. No new territories or states that came into the Union in 1850 or 1860 were included if they had not been present already as a state or territory in 1840. This procedure was followed in order to insure comparability of results from decade to decade. As a result, the totals in 1850 and 1860 differ slightly from the national trends. These differences, however, are small and do not distort the interpretation in any way. For a more complete discussion of these data, see Maris A. Vinovskis and Richard M. Bernard, "Beyond Catherine Beecher: Female Education in the Ante-Bellum Period," *Signs* 3, no. 4 (Summer 1978): 856–69. For a more general analysis of the problems of using census data, see Maris A. Vinovskis, "Problems and Opportunities in the Use of Individual and Aggregate Level Census Data," in *Historical Social Research: The Use of Historical and Process-Produced Data,* eds. Jerome M. Clubb and Erwin K. Scheuch (Stuttgart, Germany: Klett-Cotta, 1980), pp. 53–70.

9 Fishlow, "American Common School Revival." Unfortunately, most educational historians have not paid sufficient attention to the important implications of Fishlow's work.

10 For example, see Paul Boyer, *Urban Masses and Moral Order in America, 1820–1920* (Cambridge: Harvard University Press, 1978). For a good corrective to the narrow analyses of American educational development, see Lawrence A. Cremin, *American Education: The National Experience, 1783–1876* (New York: Harper and Row, 1980); Carl F. Kaestle, *Pillars of the Republic: Common Schools and American Society, 1780–1860* (New York: Hill and Wang, 1983).

11 Stephan Thernstrom, *Poverty and Progress: Social Mobility in a Nineteenth-Century City* (Cambridge: Harvard University Press, 1964), pp. 156–57.

12 Michael B. Katz and Ian E. Davey, "School Attendance and Early Industrialization in a Canadian City: A Multivariate Analysis," *History of Education Quarterly* 18, no. 3 (Fall 1978): 292.

13 Michael B. Katz, *The People of Hamilton, Canada West: Family and Class*

in a Mid-Nineteenth-Century City (Cambridge: Harvard University Press, 1975), p. 290.

14 Michael B. Katz, "Who Went to School?" *History of Education Quarterly* 12, no. 3 (Fall 1972): 432–54; Selwyn K. Troen, *The Public and the Schools: Shaping the St. Louis System, 1836–1929* (Columbia: University of Missouri Press, 1975).

15 Kaestle and Vinovskis, *Education and Social Change.*

16 On early childhood education in antebellum America, see Dean May and Maris A. Vinovskis, "A Ray of Millennial Light: Early Education and Social Reform in the Infant School Movement in Massachusetts, 1826–1840," in *Family and Kin in Urban Communities, 1700–1930,* ed. Tamara K. Hareven (New York: New Viewpoints, 1977), pp. 62–99; Carl F. Kaestle and Maris A. Vinovskis, "From Apron Strings to ABCs: Parents, Children, and Schooling in Nineteenth-Century Massachusetts," in *Turning Points: Historical and Sociological Essays on the Family,* eds. John Demos and Sarane Spence Boocock (Chicago: University of Chicago Press, 1978), pp. 39–80.

Family historians have been slow to recognize that there was a change in the way young children were treated in the first half of the nineteenth century. For example, see Carl N. Degler, *At Odds: Women and the Family in America from the Revolution to the Present* (New York: Oxford University Press, 1980), pp. 66–110. Despite such oversights, Degler's volume is the best overall analysis of the American family in the nineteenth century. For a survey of the field of American family history today, see Maris A. Vinovskis, "From Household Size to the Life Course: Some Observations on Recent Trends in Family History," *American Behavioral Scientist* 21, no. 2 (November/December 1977): 263–87; Carl N. Degler, "Women and the Family," in *The Past Before Us: Contemporary Historical Writing in the United States,* ed. Michael Kammen (Ithaca: Cornell University Press, 1980), pp. 308–26.

One of the unresolved issues is whether early education was actually a benefit or a liability for children. Historians of education have not devoted sufficient attention to speculating on the actual effects of education on children. For some exploratory essays on the impact of education on children, see Barbara Finkelstein, ed., *Regulated Children/Liberated Children: Education in Psychohistorical Perspective* (New York: Psychohistory Press, 1979).

17 Almost all of the more quantitative studies of antebellum education are focused on whites. For an introduction to the schooling of blacks in antebellum America, see Thomas L. Webber, *Deep Like the Rivers: Education in the Slave Quarter Community, 1831–1865* (New York: Norton, 1978); David Martin Ment, "Racial Segregation in the Public Schools of New England and New York, 1840–1940," unpub. Ph.D. diss. (Columbia University, 1975). Kaestle and Vinovskis, *Education and Social Change,* pp. 72–99. See also Katz and Davey, "School Attendance and Early Industrialization."

18 For an introduction to recent developments in urban studies, see Leo F. Schnore, *The New Urban History: Quantitative Explorations by American Historians* (Princeton: Princeton University Press, 1975); Kathleen Niels Con-

zen, "Community Studies, Urban History, and American Local History," in *Past Before Us,* ed. Kammen, pp. 270–91.

19 The Essex County project was initially designed and developed by Hareven and Vinovskis for 1880 and expanded back to 1860 by Kaestle and Vinovskis. For a series of studies of family life based on the Essex County data, see Tamara K. Hareven, ed., *Transitions: The Family and the Life Course in Historical Perspective* (New York: Academic Press, 1978); Tamara K. Hareven and Maris A. Vinovskis, eds., *Family and Population in Nineteenth-Century America* (Princeton: Princeton University Press, 1978).

20 Kaestle and Vinovskis, *Education and Social Change,* pp. 72–99.

21 Frank T. Denton and Peter J. George, "Social–Economic Influences on School Attendance: A Study of a Canadian County in 1871," *History of Education Quarterly* 14, no. 2 (Summer 1974): 223–32; Katz, "Reply," ibid., pp. 233–34; Frank T. Denton and Peter J. George, "Socio–Economic Influences on School Attendance: A Response to Professor Katz," ibid., 14, no. 3 (Fall 1974): 367–69. Katz was correct in criticizing the way in which Denton and George presented their multiple regressions, but he was wrong, as he has since acknowledged, in rejecting multivariate analysis altogether. Katz himself has now used multivariate analysis effectively in analyzing determinants of individual-level school attendance. See Katz and Davey, "School Attendance and Early Industrialization." Some scholars still try to analyze variations in individual-level school attendance or literacy without using multivariate analyses or adequately controlling for the effects of age. See, for example, Lee Soltow and Edward Stevens, "Economic Aspects of School Participation in Mid-Nineteenth-Century United States," *Journal of Interdisciplinary History* 8, no. 2 (Autumn 1977): 221–43.

22 Kaestle and Vinovskis, *Education and Social Change,* pp. 72–99; Katz and Davey, "School Attendance and Early Industrialization."

23 For a detailed discussion and testing of the work/consumption index, see Carl F. Kaestle and Maris A. Vinovskis, "From Fireside to Factory: School Entry and School Leaving in Nineteenth-Century Massachusetts," in *Transitions,* ed. Hareven, pp. 135–85; Karen Oppenheim Mason, Maris A. Vinovskis, and Tamara K. Hareven, "Women's Work and the Life Course in Essex County, Massachusetts, 1880," in ibid., pp. 187–216.

24 Katz and Davey tried to use the work/consumption ratio in their analysis of school attendance but found, like Kaestle and Vinovskis, that it was not a good statistical predictor. Katz and Davey, "School Attendance and Early Industrialization," 289–90.

25 Alexander Field, "Educational Expansion in Mid-Nineteenth Century Massachusetts: Human Capital Formation or Structural Reinforcement?" *Harvard Educational Review* 46, no. 4 (November 1976): 521–52, and "Industrialization and Skill Intensity: The Case of Massachusetts," *Journal of Human Recources* 15, no. 2 (Spring 1980): 149–75; Harvey Graff, *The Literacy Myth: Literacy and Social Structure in the Nineteenth-Century City* (New York: Academic Press, 1979), pp. 114–15.

26 Richard Bernard and Maris A. Vinovskis, "The Female School Teacher in Ante-Bellum Massachusetts," *Journal of Social History* 10, no. 3 (Spring 1977): 332–45. In fairness to Graff, it should be pointed out that he wanted to rerun his data using multivariate techniques but experienced unfortunate and unusual difficulties at the computer center where he was storing his data (*The Literacy Myth*, p. 76).

27 Many nineteenth-century educational advocates in America argued that schooling promoted individual social mobility, but their claims are highly exaggerated. See Maris A. Vinovskis, "Horace Mann on the Economic Productivity of Education," *New England Quarterly* 43, no. 4 (December 1970): 550–71; Carl F. Kaestle, " 'Between the Scylla of Brutal Ignorance and the Charybdis of a Literary Education': Elite Attitudes Toward Mass Schooling in the History of Education," in *Schooling and Society: Studies in the History of Education,* ed. Lawrence Stone (Baltimore: Johns Hopkins Press, 1976), pp. 177–91.

28 Alexander Field, "Educational Development and Manufacturing Development in Mid-Nineteenth Century Massachusetts," unpub. Ph.D. diss. (University of California, Berkeley, 1974), pp. 9, 52–55, 265–66, and "Educational Expansion in Massachusetts," p. 548.

29 Field, "Educational Development," 265–66.

30 Field was responding to the work of Kaestle and Vinovskis which had analyzed the length of the public school year in Massachusetts in 1860 using a different set of variables from those that Field had employed and arriving at a different interpretation from his. See Carl F. Kaestle and Maris A. Vinovskis, "Education and Social Change in Nineteenth-Century Massachusetts: Quantitative Studies," *National Institute of Education Final Report* (1976); Field, "Economic and Demographic Determinants of Educational Commitment," esp. p. 453. Although Field, in his latest publication, has shifted from his earlier position of the pivotal role of manufacturers, he has not yet explicitly confirmed and clarified such a shift in his overall interpretation.

31 Bowles and Gintis, *Schooling in Capitalist America,* pp. 174–75.

32 Kaestle and Vinovskis, *Education and Social Change,* pp. 112–25. Katz, for instance, sometimes appears to have included the development of public high schools as part of the rise of popular education. See Michael Katz, *The Irony of Early School Reform: Educational Innovation in Mid-Nineteenth-Century Massachusetts* (Cambridge: Harvard University Press, 1968). In subsequent publications, however, he identifies the rise of mass public education with the development of public educational systems rather than just increases in public school enrollment or the emergence of public high schools: Katz, "The Origins of Public Education: A Reassessment," *History of Education Quarterly* 16, no. 4 (Winter 1976): 381–407.

Much of the effort for school reform in the 1820s and 1830s, for example, was focused on creating teacher seminaries in Massachusetts. A manufacturer such as Edmund Dwight, whom Field identifies as one of the most important proponents of educational reform, anonymously contributed the large sum of

$10,000 for the creation of Normal Schools in Massachusetts. See Jonathan Messerli, *Horace Mann: A Biography* (New York: Alfred Knopf, 1972), pp. 299–300.

33 Kaestle and Vinovskis, *Education and Social Change,* pp. 208–32.

34 Ibid., p. 335. The adjusted eta² between the length of the public school year and the vote on the bill to abolish the Massachusetts Board of Education was .12. Therefore, the use of the length of the public school year as an index of support for the educational reforms of Mann is questionable.

35 Katz, *Irony of Early School Reform.*

36 Bowles and Gintis, *Schooling in Capitalist America*; Field, "Educational Development and Manufacturing Development."

CHAPTER 2

1 Michael B. Katz, *The Irony of Early School Reform: Educational Innovation in Mid-Nineteenth Century Massachusetts* (Cambridge: Harvard University Press, 1968). In subsequent work, when Katz discusses the origins of public education he focuses on the emergence of systems of public education. But even then he still says that "the date at which the first public high school opened provide a rough but convenient index of educational development." See Michael B. Katz, "The Origins of Public Education: A Reassessment," *History of Education Quarterly* 16, no. 4 (Winter 1976): 384.

2 For example, while Horace Mann was supportive of public high schools, they were only one of the many educational reforms he advocated. Jonathan Messerli, *Horace Mann: A Biography* (New York: Alfred Knopf, 1972).

3 Samuel Bowles and Herbert Gintis, *Schooling in Capitalist America: Educational Reform and the Contradictions of Economic Life* (New York: Basic Books, 1976).

4 Albert Fishlow, "The American Common School Revival: Fact or Fancy?" in *Industrialization in Two Systems: Essays in Honor of Alexander Gerschenkron,* ed. Henry Rosovsky (New York: Wiley, 1966), pp. 40–67.

Although Massachussetts probably produced the most extensive and accurate set of antebellum educational statistics, one must use them judiciously and always recognize their limitations. Throughout the text, the reported school statistics utilized have been adjusted and refined as much as possible to reflect the actual educational practices of the day. Readers who want further details on how the educational estimates were made from the annual reports should consult Carl F. Kaestle and Maris A. Vinovskis, *Education and Social Change in Nineteenth-Century Massachusetts* (Cambridge: Cambridge University Press, 1980), pp. 237–302.

The only difference between the statistical estimating procedures followed in that volume and those used in this one is the use of a more recent and reliable cost of living series. Whereas the earlier volume used the Hoover Consumer Price Index for the years 1851 to 1880 and the Federal Reserve Bank of New York Cost-of-Living Index for 1820 to 1850, this one employs the new series from Paul A. David and Peter Solar, "A Bicentenary Contribution to the History of the Cost of Living in America,"*Research in Economic History* 2 (1977): 1–80. Since the latter series was in large measure derived from the two earlier ones, in practice they are nearly identical.

5 The reader should realize that towns in New England are really townships which often include both a more densely settled area which we ordinarily call towns or villages and a less densely settled rural area. Much of the conflict over educational issues in Beverly, as we shall see, reflected the differences between the more settled portion of the township and the outlying farm areas. In 1860 Beverly had 6,154 individuals who lived in an area of approximately 8,600 acres—about two-thirds the average land area of other Massachusetts towns. The distance from the town hall in Beverly to the center of population in the Beverly Farms area, one of the most distant portions of the town, was about four miles. For details about the population and geography of the community, see Fred H. Williams, *Argument of Fred H. Williams before the Legislative Committee on Towns . . . in Favor of the Incorporation of the Town of Beverly Farms* (Boston: Daniel Gunn, 1889). Therefore, throughout the text, the reader should always remember that the town of Beverly was not a compact village but a sizable township consisting of several clusters of inhabitants, including a fairly densely populated area designated as the Grammar School district.

6 On the issue of early childhood education, see Kaestle and Vinovskis, *Education and Social Change,* pp. 46–71; Dean May and Maris A. Vinovskis, "'A Ray of Millennial Light': Early Education and Social Reform in the Infant School Movement in Massachusetts, 1826–1840," in *Family and Kin in American Urban Communities, 1800–1940,* ed. Tamara K. Hareven (New York: New Viewpoints, 1976), pp. 62–99.

Beverly School Committee, *Annual Report for 1839–40.* While public schools did not allow children under four to attend, private schools did admit young children.

7 In estimating the extent of private school enrollment, we based the figures on the number of students who relied exclusively upon the incorporated or unincorporated schools. If one also includes among the private school attendees those who used such institutions only for the one or two months intended to prolong their regular public school year, the decline in private school enrollment would be even more dramatic—from 23.5 percent in 1839–40 to 4.5 percent in 1859–60 in Beverly and from 30.9 percent in 1839–40 to 18.7 percent in 1859–60 in Salem. For a discussion of the use of private schools to prolong the common schools' year in the early 1840s, see Kaestle and Vinovskis, *Education and Social Change,* pp. 298–301.

8 Beverly School Committee, *Annual Report for 1859–60,* p. 11.

9 There were considerable fluctuations in the length of the public school year in both Beverly and Salem. In order to reflect the general trends, the extreme values of the length of the public school year were not selected for comparison purposes.

10 Alexander James Field, "Economic and Demographic Determinants of Educational Commitment: Massachusetts, 1855," *Journal of Economic History* 3, no. 2 (June 1979): 439–59.

11 Calculated from U.S. Censuses of 1840, 1850, and 1860 and the Massachusetts Census of 1855; the Beverly Auditor's Reports for 1840 and 1860; and the Massachusetts Board of Education, *Annual Reports* for 1839–40 through 1859–60. The cost of living adjustment data are from David and Solar, "A Bicentenary Contribution."

12 Calculated from Massachusetts Board of Education, *Annual Reports* for 1839–40 through 1859–60.

13 Ibid.

14 The earlier data on public school expenditures come from the Beverly School Committee Annual Reports while these data are from the Beverly Auditors' Annual Reports. Although the two sets of data are very similar, they are not always identical since the estimated school expenditures by the school committee varied somewhat from the actual expenditures reported by the auditors. For example, whereas the school committee data suggest a per capita increase in public school expenditures of 76.3 percent in the two decades prior to the Civil War, the data from the auditors reveal a 72.5 percent increase. Furthermore, the levels of expenditures according to these two different sources are nearly identical for those years.

15 Kaestle and Vinovskis, *Education and Social Change,* p. 278.

16 For further discussions of the trends in antebellum municipal expenditures, see ibid., pp. 186–207. For the most sophisticated analysis of nineteenth-century municipal expenditures, see Terrence J. McDonald, *The Parameters of Fiscal Policy in San Francisco: Socio-Economic Change, Political Culture, and Fiscal Politics, 1860–1906* (Berkeley: University of California Press, forthcoming).

17 Calculated from Massachusetts Board of Education, *Annual Report* for 1839–40 through 1859–60.

18 In Beverly, monthly wages for teachers, including value of board and adjusted for cost of living (1860 = 100), increased from $26.86 to $50.27 for males and from $8.46 to $17.42 for females. Calculated from Massachusetts Board of Education, *Annual Reports* for 1839–40 through 1859–60. Cost of living adjustment data are from David and Solar, "A Bicentenary Contribution."

19 Partly as the result of the rise in the cost of hiring teachers, Beverly as well as most other communities increasingly switched to female teachers for both the summer and winter sessions. Richard M. Bernard and Maris A. Vinovskis, "The Female School Teacher in Ante-Bellum Massachusetts," *Journal of Social History* 10, no. 3 (Spring 1977): 332–45.

20 For a discussion and analysis of the problems of rural education, see Kaestle and Vinovskis, *Education and Social Change.*

21 Katz, *Irony of Early School Reform.*

22 All of the data on the local school districts in Beverly in 1857–58 are from the Beverly School Committee, Annual Report for 1857–58.

23 Beverly Auditor's Report for 1843–44.
24 Calculated from Beverly Auditor's Report for 1843–44 and the Massachusetts Board of Education, Annual Report for 1843–44.
25 Beverly Auditor's Report for 1844–45.
26 Beverly Town Meeting Records for March 1845.
27 Beverly Town Meeting Records for March 1855.
28 Katz, *Irony of Early School Reform.*
29 Ibid. Although Katz did not emphasize the internal fights for the control of education in his discussion of Beverly, he does stress them in his analyses of other communities.
30 Ibid., p. 35.
31 Robert Rantoul, Sr., "Autobiography" (unpub. MSS, Beverly Historical Society), p. 220. Further details about Rantoul's life can be found in his diary, "Diary of Robert Rantoul," 5 vols. (unpub. MSS, Beverly Historical Society).
32 Rantoul's interest and commitment to education began as early as 1816 when he began visiting the public schools as a volunteer. He was soon elected to the Beverly School Committee where he served for four decades.

   For a more detailed and balanced analysis of Rantoul, see Arthur J. Newman, "Robert Rantoul: The Man and His Era," unpub. M.A. thesis (University of Maine, Orono, 1966). Unfortunately, the Newman thesis does not examine Rantoul's educational activities in any depth. On the need to see the close interconnection between school reformers' beliefs in Protestantism, republicanism, and capitalism, see Carl F. Kaestle, "Presidential Address—Ideology and American Educational History," *History of Education Quarterly* 22, no. 2 (Summer 1982): 123–37.
33 Katz, *Irony of Early School Reform,* p. 35.
34 Beverly Town Meeting Records, 1840–1860. The failure of Katz to stress the importance of the Beverly ministers in local educational affairs is surprising since contemporaries often mentioned it. For example, Stone's early history of Beverly observed that "for the gratifying change effected in the character of the public schools, from 1804 to 1827, the town is chiefly indebted to the school committee and especially to its chairman, Rev. Dr. Abbot, for that period, whose unwearied devotedness and careful attention to the qualifications of teachers, contributed essentially to elevate the standard of education." See Edwin M. Stone, *History of Beverly, Civil and Ecclesiastical, from Its Settlement in 1630 to 1842.* (Boston: James Munroe and Company, 1843), p. 116. Similarly, for the later period, Robert Rantoul, Sr., noted that Rev. Christopher T. Thayer "has served on the (School) Committee since his settlement in 1830 and for most of the time as chairman and has done very much more of the labor of the Committee than any other individual" (Rantoul, "Autobiography," p. 227).
35 Edwin M. Stone, *An Address Delivered in Ipswich, Mass. Before the Essex Agricultural Society at Its Twenty-Eighth Annual Exhibition, September 24, 1845* (Salem, Mass.: Gazette Office, 1846), pp. 28–29.

36 Ibid., pp. 29–30. Elsewhere Stone emphasizes the importance of public education as a way of minimizing distinctions or separations in society and of fostering republicanism. Stone, *History of Beverly,* pp. 116–17.

37 Stone was an ardent and active supporter of popular education both in Beverly and in his subsequent endeavors in Providence, Rhode Island. For a useful analysis of his varied activities, see Robert W. Lovett, "The Dual Careers of Rev. Edwin M. Stone," *Essex Institute Historical Collections* 119, no. 2 (April 1983): 81–94.

38 Christopher T. Thayer, *A Valedictory Discourse Delivered in the First Church, Beverly, July 4, 1858* (Boston: Crosby and Nichols, 1858), p. 25.

39 The distinction between ministers and laymen on the Beverly School Committee should not be drawn too sharply because often these individuals overlapped not only in their dedication to education, but in other areas as well. Robert Rantoul, Sr., for example, was deeply religious and served as a deacon of the Unitarian Church for 46 years. In 1851 he personally contributed a Bible for each of the public school districts (Rantoul, "Autobiography," p. 227). On the other hand, while most antebellum ministers were not well-to-do, some, such as Rev. Christopher T. Thayer who had inherited his fortune, were quite wealthy. On the nature and circumstances of the antebellum clergy, see Donald M. Scott, *From Office to Profession: The New England Ministry, 1750–1850* (Philadelphia: University of Pennsylvania Press, 1978).

40 Beverly School Committee, *Annual Report for 1834–44;* Massachusetts Board of Education, *Annual Report for 1844–45.*

41 Beverly Town Meeting Records for March 1845.

42 Beverly Town Meeting Records for April 1847.

43 Beverly School Committee, *Annual Report for 1852–53.*

44 Beverly Town Meeting Records for March 1852.

45 Beverly Town Meeting Records for March 1853.

46 Beverly School Committee, *Annual Report for 1853–54.*

47 By failing to act to give the power to the prudential committees, the town by default left it with the school committee. This information is in the Beverly Town Meeting Records for March 1854.

48 Beverly School Committee, *Annual Report for 1854–55.*

49 Beverly Town Meeting Records for March and April 1855.

CHAPTER 3

1 Michael B. Katz, *The Irony of Early School Reform: Educational Innovation in Mid-Nineteenth Century Massachusetts* (Cambridge: Harvard University Press, 1968).

2 Ibid., pp. 225–69. The analysis of Massachusetts communities that did or did not establish a public high school in 1840 or 1865 is based upon only a small subsample of the cities and towns in that state. By not taking into consideration the dates when the high schools were established, Katz fails to see the dynamics of this system. Furthermore, rather than having relied upon simple

correlation or factor analysis, Katz should have used some form of multivariate analysis with the establishment of the high school as the dependent variable.

3 On Massachusetts colonial education, see James Axtell, *The School Upon a Hill: Education and Society in Colonial New England* (New Haven: Yale University Press, 1974); Lawrence A. Cremin, *American Education: The Colonial Experience, 1607–1787* (New York: Harper and Row, 1970); Geraldine Joanne Murphy, "Massachusetts Bay Colony: The Role of Government in Education" (unpub. Ph.D. diss., Radcliffe College, 1960).

4 Alexander James Inglis, *The Rise of the High School in Massachusetts* (New York: Teachers College, 1911). The Inglis volume is still the best book on the legal aspects of Massachusetts secondary education in the colonial and early national periods. The more recent attempt by Sylvia Clark to investigate Massachusetts nineteenth-century legislation in regard to education is neither very analytical nor particularly useful. Sylvia Marie Clark, "James Gordon Carter: His Influence in Massachusetts Education, History, and Politics from 1820–1850" (unpub. Ph.D. diss., Boston College, 1982).

5 On the early history of Beverly education, see Edwin M. Stone, *History of Beverly, Civil and Ecclesiastical, from its Settlement in 1630 to 1842* (Boston: James Munroe and Company, 1843), pp. 110–19.

6 Inglis, *Rise of the High School in Massachusetts,* pp. 27–28.

7 On the development of public high schools partly as a reaction to the growth of private academies in the early nineteenth century, see Emit Duncan Grizzell, *Origin and Development of the High School in New England before 1865* (New York: Macmillan Company, 1923); Silas Hertzler, *The Rise of the Public High School in Connecticut* (Baltimore: Warwick and York, 1930); Inglis, *Rise of the High School in Massachusetts*; Theodore R. Sizer, ed., *The Age of the Academies* (New York: Teachers College, 1964).

8 Inglis, *Rise of the High School in Massachusetts.*

9 The dates of the establishment of public high schools in Massachusetts are from Inglis, *Rise of the High School in Massachusetts,* pp. 42–45, and Grizzell, *Origins and Development of the High School,* pp. 94, 132, 147–49. It should be remembered that some of the dates of the establishment are quite tentative and that a few of the towns abandoned their public high schools soon after they were opened.

10 Stone, *History of Beverly,* pp. 118–19. In 1837 another private academy was incorporated in Beverly as the New England Christian Academy under Joseph Henry Siewers as a sectarian school based upon the manual labor system. Due to economic difficulties, the New England Christian Academy closed within two years.

11 Frederick A. Ober, "Beverly," in *History of Essex County, Massachusetts with Biographical Sketches of Many of the Pioneers and Prominent Men,* ed. Hamilton Hurd (Philadelphia: J. W. Lewis and Company, 1888), pp. 721–22.

12 Scattered comments in unpublished Annual Reports of the Beverly School Committee to the Massachusetts Board of Education located in the Massachusetts State Library.

Whereas Katz found great opposition to the private academy in Groton, there does not appear to have been any particular hostility directed to the Beverly Academy initially. See Katz, *Irony of Early School Reform,* pp. 62–80.

13 Inglis, *Rise of the High School in Massachusetts,* p. 30.

14 Gloucester School Committee Annual Report cited in Massachusetts Board of Education, *Annual Report for 1838–39* (Boston: Dutton and Wentworth, 1839), p. 18.

15 Inglis, *Rise of the High School in Massachusetts,* p. 30.

16 Interestingly, when the Haverhill School Committee was arguing for the establishment of a public high school, it not only cited the legal requirement but also the opposition to one among the outlying school districts. Massachusetts Board of Education, *Annual Report for 1839–40* (Boston: Dutton and Wentworth, 1840), pp. 18–21. The division between the supporters of a public high school in the center district and their opponents in the outlying districts, a common theme among Massachusetts communities, proves to have played an important role in the debates over the high school in Beverly, too.

17 Beverly Town Meeting Records, March and April 1844.

Part of the impetus for the establishment of a public high school at this time may be due to the split among the trustees of the Beverly Academy over the hiring of James W. Boyden as the principal. Robert Rantoul, one of the founders of the Beverly Academy, resigned from the Board of Trustees in protest. Robert Rantoul, Sr., "Autobiography," MSS in the Beverly Historical Society, pp. 221–23.

18 In 1850 towns with less than 8,000 inhabitants were excused from maintaining high schools if at least two of their district schools provided certain subjects in their curricula. Few communities, however, seemed to take advantage of this provision. In 1857 this exception was also repealed. Inglis, *Rise of the High School in Massachusetts,* pp. 30–31.

19 On educational reforms in Massachusetts during these years, see Frederick M. Binder, *The Age of the Common School, 1830–1865* (New York: John Wiley and Sons, 1974); Raymond B. Culver, *Horace Mann and Religion in the Massachusetts Public Schools* (New Haven: Yale University Press, 1929); Alexander Field, "Educational Reform and Manufacturing Development in Mid-Nineteenth-Century Massachusetts" (unpub. Ph.D. diss., University of California, Berkeley, 1974); Mary McDougall Gordon, "Union with a Virtuous Past: The Development of School Reform in Massachusetts, 1789–1837" (unpub. Ph.D. diss. University of Pittsburgh, 1974); Carl F. Kaestle, *Pillars of the Republic: Common Schools and American Society, 1780–1860* (New York: John Wiley and Sons, 1983); Carl F. Kaestle and Maris A. Vinovskis, *Education and Social Change in Nineteenth-Century Massachusetts* (Cambridge: Cambridge University Press, 1980); Katz, *Irony of Early School Reform.*

20 One possible explanation for the new interest in public education in the early 1850s is that it was part of the Protestant reaction against the growing establishment of private schools for Catholic children. Indeed, Katz argues

that in Lawrence some of the impetus for public schooling in the mid-1850s was caused by the fear among Protestants of parochial schools (*Irony of Early School Reform,* pp. 93–112).

While the reactions against the threats perceived to be posed by the increase of foreign-born residents in Massachusetts and by their efforts to establish Catholic schools may have played some role in persuading citizens in Beverly to push for more public education, it is unlikely that this factor played a major role in 1853 and 1854 since the proportion of foreign-born persons in the community was much smaller than in most other cities and a Catholic Church was not established there until after the Civil War. Furthermore, there is no indication in the local newspaper or the school committee reports that the fear of Catholics and their parochial schools was a major consideration. On the animosity between Catholics and Protestants during these years, see Oscar Handlin, *Boston's Immigrants: A Study in Acculturation,* enlarged edition (New York: Atheneum, 1968). While many Protestants were convinced that the Catholic Church in Massachusetts placed a very high priority on establishing parochial schools, John Fitzpatrick, Bishop of Boston, was accused by other Catholic leaders of being much too lax in encouraging and developing such facilities for Catholic students. Thomas H. O'Connor, *Fitzpatrick's Boston, 1846–1866* (Boston: Northeastern University Press, 1984).

21 Beverly Town Meeting Records, March 1853.

22 Beverly Town Meeting Records, March 1854.

23 Beverly *Citizen,* February 9, 1854.

24 Beverly *Citizen,* March 4, 1854.

25 Beverly Town Meeting Records, March and April 1854.

26 Beverly *Citizen,* April 9, 16, and 23, 1853. Katz does say that Rantoul "formally retired from town affairs" in 1854, but he does not seem to be aware of the Maxey scandal or the fact that Rantoul does not appear to have been a major contributor to the effort to establish a public high school in the early 1850s. Katz is correct, however, in pointing out that Rantoul did speak on behalf of the proposed public high school in 1857 (*Irony of Early School Reform,* pp. 26–27.

27 Beverly Town Meeting Records, March 1854.

28 Beverly *Citizen,* March 4, 1854.

29 Beverly Town Meeting Records, April 1854.

30 Records of the Beverly School Committee, March 10, 1855.

In the school report for that year, the superintendent made it clear that even though the town had allocated more money for the common schools instead of a public high school, there was still a pressing need for this institution of higher education—especially as a stimulus for improvements among the students in the common schools. See Beverly School Committee, *Annual Report for 1854–55.*

31 Beverly *Citizen,* April 14, 1854.

32 The anger over the actions of the school committee probably had more to do with its supposed usurpation of power rather than the issue of the high school.

Five of the twelve members elected to the school committee in March 1855 had been members of the Special Committee on the Public High School the year before, and three of these five had called for the establishment of that institution. See Beverly Town Meeting Records, April 1854 and March 1855.

One might argue that the wholesale replacement of the members of the former Beverly School Committee in March 1855 was only one part of several larger political changes in Beverly as a result of the unexpected surge of support for the American Party (the "Know-Nothings") throughout the state. Indeed, while almost all of the Beverly selectmen had been reelected annually since 1850, in 1855 all five selectmen were replaced, and 52.1 percent of Beverly voters in the subsequent November balloting for governor supported the American Party candidate, Henry J. Gardner.

While the appearance and success of the American Party undoubtedly contributed to the willingness of some Beverly citizens to replace all previous municipal office holders, most voters did not endorse such sweeping changes, and many former officials were reelected in 1855. In addition, since the American Party generally appears to have been strongly supportive of public education, it is unlikely that it would have targeted the strongest supporters of public schooling for replacement. Finally, since the newly elected school committee members resigned in protest and were then replaced by many of the previous members one month later, it is unlikely that the controversy over the actions of the Beverly School Committee of 1854 was caused by the appearance of the American Party in Beverly.

On the impact of the American Party on Massachusetts politics, see John Raymond Mulkern, "The Know-Nothing Party in Massachusetts," unpub. Ph.D. diss. (Boston University, 1963). William Gienapp is now in the process of analyzing the position of political parties in the 1850s on education and has raised some very important questions about earlier interpretations of the American Party. William Gienapp, "Who Were the Northern Know-Nothings?" Paper presented at the Social Science History Association Meeting, Toronto, October 1984.

33 Beverly Town Meeting Records, April 1855.

34 Ibid.

35 Beverly Town Meeting Records, July 1855.

36 Beverly Town Meeting Records, April 1856 and March 1857. The subsequent debate on this matter indicates that the supporters of the public high school were by no means unanimous about the ideals of educational reform in Beverly. W. C. Boyden and C. T. Thayer, strong advocates of the public high school, were among those in the 1856 town meeting who tried to rescind the previously adopted resolution to supply the schools with books and stationery while John I. Baker, also a prominent supporter of the public high school, argued against them.

37 Beverly Town Meeting Records, March and April 1856.

38 Ibid.

39 Beverly Town Meeting Records, December 1856.

40 Beverly Town Meeting Records, March 1857. Albert Boyden, *Here and There in the Family Tree* (Salem, 1949). p. 22.
41 Beverly Town Meeting Records, July 1857. In May 1857 the legislature repealed the law of 1850 which had exempted towns with fewer than 8,000 inhabitants from maintaining a public high school if they met certain conditions. Inglis, *Rise of the High School in Massachusetts,* p. 32. The repeal of this possible exemption, however, does not appear to have precipitated agitation on behalf of a public high school since the proceedings were already underway before the new legislation was enacted.
42 Beverly Town Meeting Records, July 1857.
43 Beverly Town Meeting Records, September 1857.
44 Beverly Town Meeting Records, October 1857.
45 *Annual Report of the School Committee for the Town of Beverly,* March 1859, p. 5.

CHAPTER 4

1 Beverly School Committee, *Annual Report for 1857–58,* pp. 10–12.
2 Ibid., p. 6.
3 Ibid., p. 4.
4 Ibid., pp. 11–12.
5 Beverly Town Meeting Records for March 1858.
6 Beverly School Committee, *Annual Report for 1858–59,* p. 5. The records do not indicate how many children took and passed the qualifying examinations for entrance into the high school. The number taking the exam probably was not much larger than the number entering as there was no discussion of the problems of preparation for the high school in either the school reports or the local newspaper.
7 Calculated from ibid.
8 Ibid., p. 6.
9 Beverly Town Meeting Records for March 1859.
10 Beverly School Committee, *Annual Report for 1859–60,* p. 6.
11 Calculated from ibid., p. 32; Massachusetts Board of Education, *Annual Report for 1858–59.*
12 Beverly *Citizen,* November 10, 1858.
   In his analysis, Katz claims that by the eve of the Civil War, Beverly was developing into a "one-industry" town producing shoes (Katz, *Irony of Early School Reform,* pp. 81–82). While Katz is correct that shoemaking was one of the major industries in the community, he may have underestimated the importance of other economic activities. For example, according to the federal manuscript census of industries for 1860, boot and shoemaking in Beverly employed 34.4 percent of the male workers, utilized 18.3 percent of the capital, and constituted 42.0 percent of the value of goods produced.
   Codfishing used more than twice as much capital as boot and shoemaking but produced less than half the value of products. Whereas 355 males were

employed in boot and shoemaking, 485 were in codfishing. See U.S. Manuscript Census of Industries for 1860.

Similarly, if one looks at the value of goods produced according to the state census of industries in 1855, boot and shoemaking accounted for 19.5 percent of the total products, while codfishing resulted in 12.4 percent, and chair and cabinet manufacturing 10.3 percent of the total. The smaller proportion of the total goods produced by boot and shoemaking in 1855 than in 1860 is less due to the expansion of that industry during those five years than the fact that the state survey included agricultural and other small manufacturing efforts as well. Francis DeWitt, *Statistical Information Relating to Certain Branches of Industry of Massachusetts for 1855* (Boston: William White, 1856), pp. 115–17.

The data on industries in Beverly are undoubtedly limited both in terms of their coverage and accuracy. Nevertheless, it is probably misleading to emphasize the boot and shoemakers without acknowledging the importance of other economic activities within that community. For a contemporary discussion of the rise of the boot and shoe industry in Beverly, see William C. Morgan, *Shoes and Shoemaking: A Brief Sketch of the History and Manufacture of Shoes from the Earliest Time* (Beverly, Mass.: Kehew and Odell, 1897).

13 Beverly Town Meeting Records, February 1860.

14 Beverly *Citizen,* March 3, 1860.

15 Beverly Town Meeting Records, March 1860.

16 Ibid.

17 Ibid. Joseph Thissell had served as an assessor for the town in 1857 and 1858 but was not one of the prominent or frequent local office holders. Apparently he was not a member of any of the churches in Beverly.

18 Ibid.

19 Whereas Katz was able to match the census, tax, and voting records of 343 of the 392 voters, this study, utilizing other types of information as well as reflecting repeated searches for linkages, matched 370 of these records. See Katz, *The Irony of Early School Reform.*

Despite the use of a greater number and variety of records on mid-nineteenth-century Beverly citizens, there are still instances where one is not certain of the validity of the record linkage. For example, while in many cases an exact link was made easier by the availability of the middle initials of the subject, in other situations this information was not furnished. Therefore, each of the 370 matched cases in this analysis were coded for reliability of the linkage. Then analyses were performed to determine if the inclusion of linked data based on less conclusive evidence affected the findings. The results of this inquiry into the potential distortions due to the linkage did not indicate any particular biases.

The reader should also remember throughout this analysis that although the data used in Katz's study and in this investigation are similar in type, they are not identical since he matched only 87.5 percent of the voters whereas this analysis matched 94.4 percent. Since it was not possible to compare the two lists of matched voters, one cannot be certain of how much, if any, of the differences in the results of this reanalysis are due to the additional 27 voters included in this study.

20 The newspaper account of the meeting mentioned "a large portion of the voters remaining silent when their names were called" (Beverly *Citizen,* March 17, 1860). It is impossible to ascertain exactly how many voters abstained, but one suspects that it may not have been as large as suggested in the newspaper story since the total number of voters on the other issues that same day was even smaller. See Beverly Town Meeting Records, March 1860.

21 Calculated from Beverly Tax Valuation List for 1859 and the Beverly Town Meeting Records, March 1860.

22 Katz, *Irony of Early School Reform.*

23 For an excellent introduction to multiple classification analysis, see Frank M. Andrews, J. N. Morgan, John A. Sonquist, and Laura Klem, *Multiple Classification Analysis,* 2d edition (Ann Arbor, Mich.: Institute for Social Research, 1973).

24 Katz, *Irony of Early School Reform,* p. 85.

25 Ibid., pp. 21, 275.

26 For some notable exceptions, see Carl F. Kaestle, *Pillars of the Republic: Common Schools and American Society, 1780–1860* (New York: Hill and Wang, 1983); David Tyack, "The Kingdom of God and the Common School: Protestant Ministers and the Educational Awakening in the West," *Harvard Educational Review* 36, no. 4 (Fall, 1966): 447–69; David Tyack and Elisabeth Hansot, *Managers of Virtue: Public School Leadership in America, 1820–1980* (New York: Basic Books, 1982).

27 Katz, *Irony of Early School Reform,* p. 35.

28 Beverly *Citizen,* March 24, 1860.

29 The records of the various churches were gathered from published and unpublished lists of their members as well as records of their financial contributions to the church. Only in the case of the Second Congregational Church was it impossible to obtain membership or subscription lists, and therefore it was necessary to rely upon lists of church officers. Fortunately, from the perspective of the completeness of the records, the Second Congregational Church in the 1850s was in such disarray that it had few adherents. Therefore, the list of church lay officials for that institution probably represented most of the male members anyway. For a comprehensive and thoughtful analysis of the Second Congregational Church, see Robert W. Lovett, "A Parish Divided and Reunited, The Precinct of Salem and Beverly, 1813–1903," *Essex Institute Historical Collections* 99, no. 3 (July 1863): 57–90.

30 In considering the variations among the congregations, it is important to recognize that some of these, especially for the Second and Fourth Congregational Churches, are based upon very few individuals and therefore subject to the obvious limitations imposed by any generalizations based upon small numbers. Nevertheless, the results are sufficiently interesting and perhaps

useful for future comparisons because the data were presented by individual churches rather than grouped together.

31 Raymond B. Culver, *Horace Mann and Religion in the Massachusetts Public Schools* (New Haven: Yale University Press, 1929).

32 Unitarians were likely to be residents of the central districts, affluent, and active and successful participants in local politics.

33 Lovett, "A Parish Divided and Reunited."

34 Herman C. Johnson, *Centenary Handbook of the Washington Street Congregational Church* (Beverly, Mass.: Charles R. Piper, 1937).

35 For a detailed and very useful analysis of the Second Baptist Church, see Mark E. Lindh, *A Sesquicentennial History of North Shore Community Baptist Church, 1829–1879* (Wenham, Mass.: Gordon College Press, 1979).

36 Ibid.

37 Katz, *Irony of Early School Reform,* p. 85.

38 Ibid., p. 21.

39 Ibid., pp. 21–22, 84. One of the problems in making any inferences between personal and real estate holdings is that it was much easier to hide personal holdings than it was to hide real estate one owned. Indeed, now there are clear indications that throughout the nineteenth century personal wealth was hidden. On the accuracy of the valuations, see Henry P. Moulton, *Arguments and Testimony in Behalf of the Town of Beverly Against the Division of the Town before the Legislative Committee on Towns, 1888* (Boston: Rand Avery, 1888).

40 Apparently Katz used the tax records for 1860. These, however, could not be located in the Beverly City Hall due in part to the disorganized condition of the old tax records in its basement vault. Therefore, the 1859 data were used instead.

41 Katz used three categories of wealth—real, personal, and total. Each of these categories was then subdivided into three different levels of wealth. From his table, however, one cannot ascertain what proportion of total wealth was invested in personal or real wealth (*Irony of Early School Reform,* p. 276). Since it was important to try to represent both the amount and type of wealth in one variable for the MCA, this analysis used a slightly different operationalization of this factor than the one employed by Katz.

42 Based upon another MCA run not reported here which used only the amount, but not the type of wealth. The wealth variable subdivided by type of property was a stronger predictor of voting behavior than the wealth variable by itself.

The questioning of whether the least wealthy were the most likely to oppose the high school is suggested by Sylvia Olfson Shapiro, "Sources of Equality: Social Theory, Social History and Educational Policy," unpub. Ph.D. diss. (Harvard University, 1981), pp. 66–71.

43 Katz, *Irony of Early School Reform,* pp. 21–22, 85. Since the publication of this work, Katz has moved away from looking at several groups of occupations. Now he advocates subdividing everyone into either the business or the worker classes. Michael B. Katz, "Social Class in North American Urban

History," *Journal of Interdisciplinary History* 11, no. 4 (Spring 1981): 579–605; Michael B. Katz, M¹ ¹ael J. Doucet and Mark J. Stern, *The Social Organization of Early Industrial Capitalism* (Cambridge: Harvard University Press, 1982).

The division of individuals into two classes is unsatisfactory conceptually and statistically. Katz dichotomizes occupations in a way that does not reflect either the perceptions or behavior of most mid-nineteenth-century Americans. Furthermore, by sacrificing the more detailed occupational groupings, he underutilizes the available information. Thus, while Katz should be commended for trying to develop a more theoretical approach to class analysis, the results are too simplistic and not particularly useful. For critiques of his most recent work, see Maris A. Vinovskis, "Searching for Classes in Urban North America," *Journal of Urban History* (forthcoming); Alexander J. Field, "Review," *Journal of Interdisciplinary History* 14, no. 3 (Winter 1984): 669–701.

44 Katz, *Irony of Early School Reform,* pp. 20–21.

45 Ibid., p. 22.

46 Ibid., pp. 39, 271. This inconsistency in the treatment of farmers is pointed out by Shapiro, "Sources of Equality," pp. 64–65.

47 After examining a set of MCAs with each of the independent variables removed one at a time, it appears that controlling for geography is the major reason for the large reduction in the relative hostility of the farmers as an occupational subgroup.

48 Katz, *Irony of Early School Reform,* pp. 21–22, 80–86.

49 One should not, however, draw too sharp a distinction between the shoemakers and the fishermen or mariners in Beverly since during periods of economic downturn in the shoe industry, many of the younger shoemakers would seek temporary employment as fishermen or mariners. The problem in the late 1850s was that both shoemaking and fishing were economically depressed at the same time in Beverly.

50 Ibid., p. 80.

51 Since he did not find any written records by the shoemakers and claimed that the "timid town newspaper tried to pretend that the strike did not exist," Katz relied on the Lynn newspapers for the attitude of the strikers (*Irony of Early School Reform,* p. 81). Consulting the Lynn newspapers for information about the shoemakers on strike can be helpful, but it obviously does not speak directly to the reactions of Beverly shoe workers to the Beverly High School. Furthermore, the Beverly *Citizen* provided considerable information about the Beverly shoe strike which Katz should have incorporated into his analysis.

Since there are no contemporary mentions of any connection between the strike and the negative vote on the high school in either the discussions about the strike or the vote on the high school, one should be extremely cautious about making such a strong linkage between them.

52 Ibid., p. 84.

53 For analyses of the Lynn shoe strike, see Alan Dawley, *Class and Community: The Industrial Revolution in Lynn* (Cambridge: Harvard University Press, 1976), pp. 78–89; Paul G. Faler, *Mechanics and Manufacturers in the Early Industrial Revolution: Lynn, Massachusetts, 1780-1981,* pp. 222–33. For a very perceptive and useful critique of the works of Dawley and Faler, see Friedrich Langer, "Class, Culture, and Class Consciousness in Ante-bellum Lynn: A Critique of Alan Dawley and Paul Faler," *Social History* 6, no. 3 (October 1981): 317–32.

54 Philip S. Foner, *History of the Labor Movement in the United States,* vol. 1 (New York: International Publishers, 1947), pp. 241–45.

55 In the various accounts of the strike, including those by newspapers sympathetic to the strike, Beverly is not mentioned among those communities which supported the strike in February. Among the newspapers consulted were the Beverly *Citizen, Salem Register, Salem Gazette, Salem Observer,* Essex County *Mercury, Lynn Bay State, Lynn Weekly Reporter, Lynn News, Boston Daily Evening Transcript, Boston Post,* and *Boston Daily Advertiser.*

56 Beverly *Citizen,* March 2 and 10, 1860.

57 Ibid., March 17, 1860.

58 *Salem Gazette,* March 20, 1860.

59 Beverly *Citizen,* March 10 and 17, 1860. Even in Lynn some of the merchants and manufacturers supported the strike and pledged contributions to the strike fund. See Dawley, *Class and Community,* pp. 83–85, 88–89.

60 Faler, *Mechanics and Manufacturers,* pp. 222–33.

61 Beverly *Citizen,* March 17, 1860. Faler, unlike Katz, recognized that "the bulk of the people in many towns felt more in common with the shoemakers than with the bosses" (Faler, *Mechanics and Manufacturers,* p. 228). The local support for shoemakers is not surprising since their sheer numbers in many communities guaranteed them much popular support from relatives and neighbors. Even in Lynn, the manufacturers who opposed the strike found it necessary to call upon outside police assistance to defend their property.

62 Ibid. The Beverly *Citizen* was sympathetic to the strike and presented the actions of the strikers in Beverly and elsewhere in a very favorable light.

Although the March 17 issue expressed doubt that the manufacturers would sign a bill of prices or wages, later James Dillon of Lynn, in addressing the Beverly strikers, said that 23 of the manufacturers had signed the Bill of Wages (*Salem Gazette,* March 27, 1860). Unfortunately, it is not clear from the newspaper account whether he meant 23 of the Beverly shoe manufacturers or of those in the general area. In any case, few shoe manufacturers agreed to the demands and the strike collapsed by the end of April.

63 Beverly *Citizen,* March 10 and 24, 1860.

64 Interestingly, very few of the Beverly strike leaders identified in the local newspaper voted on the high school. However, Stephen M. Furbush, a shoemaker with only $100 personal property according to the census, acted as the secretary at one of the early strike meetings in Beverly and voted for the high

school two weeks later (Beverly *Citizen,* March 3, 1860). Lists of the supporters of the strike in Beverly were produced because there are reports of several hundred workers signing various bills of wages. Unfortunately, none of these general lists of the Beverly strikers have been located despite an extensive search in various local historical societies.

In addition to the Beverly *Citizen, The Salem Register, Salem Gazette, Salem Observer,* Essex County *Mercury, Lynn Bay State, Lynn News, Lynn Reporter, Boston Post, Boston Daily Advertiser,* and *Boston Daily Evening Transcript* were examined for information about the shoe strike.

65 Katz, *Irony of Early School Reform,* p. 31.

66 Carl F. Kaestle and Maris A. Vinovskis, *Education and Social Change in Nineteenth-Century Massachusetts* (Cambridge: Cambridge University Press, 1980), pp. 208–32.

67 A separate MCA was run using early party affiliation instead of current party affiliation as the independent variable.

68 Although the Beverly *Citizen* was supportive of the Republicans in 1860, it did publish lists of local Democratic Party activists as well as those of Republicans. Given the efforts by both parties in 1860 to identify publicly as many individuals with themselves as possible, one can assemble political affiliations for a considerable number of voters in that community from the newspaper lists.

69 Beverly *Citizen,* March 10, 1860.

70 Prior to 1858 the elections for the school committee were only for one year. In 1858 the school committee positions were changed to three-year terms— probably reflecting the attempt by some in the community to protect the members from immediate retaliation at the next town meeting.

71 An analysis of all Beverly officials from 1854 to 1860 indicates that most of the people on the Citizen's Ticket were long-established members of the political elite in Beverly and represented most of the churches in that community. While a few Democrats were on the list, most of the others, especially for the top offices, were Republicans. The Citizen's Ticket did not endorse individuals for the lower-level positions such as the surveyors of the highways or fence viewers.

72 The exceptions in the Beverly election were for the positions of inspector of the police, a member of the school board, and a member of the Board of Health. In Lynn, however, where the shoe workers organized themselves politically six months after the strike, they won control of nearly every position in the city government (Faler, *Mechanics and Manufacturers,* p. 230). This difference in the political events in the two communities reinforces my suspicion that Katz has exaggerated the extent of divisions within Beverly during the strike.

73 Given some of the apparent strong antagonism to the ministers on the school committee for forcing the high school upon a reluctant community, it is surprising that voters continued to elect four more ministers at the same meeting

when they voted against the high school. This may reflect the dilemma that many mid-nineteenth-century voters faced. Although they did not always agree with the recommendations of the clergymen on the local school committees, the place of ministers on these committees was assumed except under very extraordinary circumstances such as the mid–1850s in Beverly when the town meeting tried to eliminate temporarily the role of the clergymen on the school committee.

74 These data were obtained from the Beverly Town Meeting Records for those years.

75 The scale was constructed on the basis of an estimate of the prestige and importance attached to these offices by contemporaries. Since the amount of information available for constructing this scale is very limited, the relative weights assigned should be regarded as only very crude estimates.

76 In order to see if the introduction of weights for the offices may have seriously distorted the results, another MCA was run using the total number of offices held (unweighted). The results were virtually identical, but the weighted version of this variable was kept in the final MCA run because it is more appropriate conceptually than the unweighted one.

77 Several readers of a preliminary draft of this manuscript who are not familiar with the multiple classification analysis have wondered whether the great importance of geography as an independent variable is not simply because of its overlap with other factors such as occupation or wealth. To some extent, of course, geography and other variables do overlap. But the degree of that interaction is not very large if one looks at the bivariate tables of those variables. In addition, whereas the simple relationships (eta^2) between the vote on the Beverly High School for occupation and wealth are only .0547 and .0761 respectively, the relationship is .1795 for geographic area. Similarly, if occupation is removed from the multiple classification analysis, the overall explanatory power of the equation (R^2) is actually increased by .0103 due to the reduction in the number of categories while it is decreased by .0384 by the exclusion of wealth as an independent variable. The removal of geographic area as an independent variable, on the other hand, reduces the adjusted R^2 by .0847. In addition, if geographic area is removed as an independent variable, the importance of either wealth or occupation, as measured by the beta values, is not greatly enhanced. Finally, and perhaps most significantly, the relative importance of the independent variables (after controlling for the effects of each one) is indicated by the beta values, which show a greater importance of geographic area as a predictor of the vote on the Beverly High School than any of the other variables. In other words, despite some overlap between where a voter lived and his other characteristics, there is little reason either statistically or historically to doubt the importance of geographic location as a predictor of his vote on the high school in March 1860.

78 Katz, *Irony of Early School Reform*, p. 85.

79 Ibid., p. 79. Ravitch criticized Katz for his failure to acknowledge the impor-

tance of geography in determining the vote on the high school. Diane Ravitch, *The Revisionists Revised: A Critique of the Radical Attacks on the Schools* (New York: Basic Books, 1978), p. 120.

80 Frederick A. Ober, "Beverly" in *History of Essex County, Massachusetts with Biographical Sketches of Many of the Pioneers and Prominent Men,* ed. D. Hamilton Hurd, vol. 1 (Philadelphia: A. W. Lewis, 1888), p. 739. Although Katz consulted the Ober account, for some reason he did not use this very important nineteenth-century description of the struggle over the high school.

81 Beverly *Citizen,* February 23, 1861.

82 Ibid., March 2, 1861.

83 Ibid., March 9, 1861.

84 Beverly Town Records, March 1861.

85 Beverly *Citizen,* March 16, 1861.

86 Ibid., April 6, 1861.

87 Beverly Town Meeting Records, April 1861.

88 Beverly School Committee, *Annual Report for 1861–62,* p. 6.

89 Interestingly, when the area of Beverly Farms tried to secede from the town and become incorporated as a separate community in the late 1880s, one of the reasons frequently cited was the difficulty for children in the outlying areas to attend the Beverly High School which was now located in the densely populated part of the town. See Fred H. Williams, *Arguments of Fred H. Williams and Testimony of Petitioners and Remonstrants Presented before the Committee on Towns of the Massachusetts Legislature Relative to the Incorporation of the Town of "Beverly Farms,"* January 20 to February 8, 1886. Perhaps somewhat ironically, the residents of the Beverly Farms area had enjoyed the presence of the high school in their neighborhood on the eve of the Civil War, but they nonetheless had voted against its continuance.

The attempt to establish the Beverly Farms area as a separate and independent town in the late 1880s was generated to a large extent by the influx of wealthy outsiders, but the fact that almost all taxpayers of that area signed and supported the petition reinforces the impression that many residents of the outlying areas did not identify themselves with the interests and needs of the central part of the more settled town of Beverly. For a discussion of the effort to separate Beverly into two communities, see Richard Harmond, "The Time They Tried to Divide Beverly," *Essex Institute Historical Collections,* 104, no. 1 (January 1968): 19–33.

90 Based upon two additional MCAs using the three best independent variables according to Katz or myself.

CONCLUSION

1 Michael Katz, *The Irony of Early School Reform: Educational Innovation in Mid-Nineteenth Century Massachusetts* (Cambridge: Harvard University Press, 1968).

2 Katz emphasizes the socioeconomic dislocations in the community during the 1850s as a major factor for the unrest in that town (*Irony of Early School*

Reform, pp. 80–81). While he is correct that Beverly, like most other towns in the Commonwealth, was experiencing changes, perhaps he exaggerated the extent or severity of them in Beverly.

The population of Beverly grew from 4,689 in 1840 to 5,376 in 1850, 5,944 in 1855, and 6,154 in 1860. Thus, the period 1850–55 witnessed the highest annual rate of growth. Yet the rate of population increase in both Essex County and Massachusetts as a whole was considerably higher than in Beverly. Furthermore, the percentage of foreign-born residents in Beverly was much less than in most other urban areas, and only about half of them were from Ireland. Calculated from U.S. Population Censuses of 1840, 1850, and 1860 and the Massachusetts State Census of 1855.

In addition, Katz stresses increased mechanization of shoemaking in Beverly in the 1850s and 1860s as the introduction of machines increased output and reduced the need for skilled workers (*Irony of the Early School Reform,* p. 81). While Katz is correct in pointing to the changes in shoemaking, especially the introduction of devices for cutting and rolling leather, perhaps he has exaggerated the extent of mechanization of that industry in Beverly on the eve of the Civil War. For the 500 male and female shoeworkers listed in the federal manuscript census of industries in 1860, there were only 25 stitching machines available (U.S. Manuscript Census of Industries for 1860). On the mechanization of the shoe industry and its effects on the workers and their families, see William H. Mulligan, Jr., "Mechanization and Work in the American Shoe Industry: Lynn, Massachusetts, 1852–1883," *Journal of Economic History* 41, no. 1 (March 1981): 59–83; William H. Mulligan, Jr., "Mechanizing the Gentle Craft: The Introduction of Machinery into the Lynn Massachusetts Shoe Industry, 1852–1883," in *Essays from the Lowell Conference on Industrial History, 1980 and 1981,* eds. Robert Weible, Oliver Ford, and Paul Marion (Lowell, Mass.: Lowell Conference on Industrial History, 1981), pp. 33–45.

3 Jonathan Messerli, *Horace Mann: A Biography* (New York: Alfred A. Knopf, 1972).

4 Carl F. Kaestle and Maris A. Vinovskis, *Education and Social Change in Nineteenth-Century Massachusetts* (Cambridge: Cambridge University Press, 1980), pp. 208–32.

5 At first the secretaries of the Massachusetts Board of Education were unwilling to use the state law to coerce towns to establish public high schools. Over the years, however, political conditions changed, and in 1865 they began to threaten those towns that were required to maintain high schools with the loss of state funds if they failed to comply (Katz, *Irony of Early School Reform,* p. 15).

6 On Massachusetts education in the late nineteenth and early twentieth centuries, see Marvin Lazerson, *Origins of the Urban School: Public Education in Massachusetts, 1870–1915* (Cambridge: Harvard University Press, 1971).

7 In the mid-1860s Beverly abandoned its local school district system and consolidated schools under the control of the Town School Committee.

8 Katz, *Irony of Early School Reforms*; Samuel Bowles and Herbert Gintis, *Schooling in Capitalist America* (New York: Basic Books, 1976).

9 Carl F. Kaestle, *Pillars of the Republic: Common Schools and American Society, 1780–1860* (New York: Hill and Wang, 1983); David Tyack, "The Kingdom of God and the Common School: Protestant Ministers and the Educational Awakening in the West," *Harvard Educational Review* 36, no. 4 (Fall 1966): 447–69; David Tyack and Elisabeth Hansot, *Managers of Virtue: Public School Leadership in America, 1820–1980* (New York: Basic Books, 1982).

10 For historians who have noted the involvement of nineteenth-century ministers in education, see Timothy L. Smith, *Revivalism & Social Reform: American Protestantism on the Eve of the Civil War* (New York: Abingdon Press, 1957) and Clifford S. Griffin, *Their Brothers' Keepers: Moral Stewardship in the United States, 1800–1865* (New Brunswick, N.J.: Rutgers University Press, 1960). For scholars of the ministry who have ignored the role of the clergy in school affairs, see Donald M. Scott, *From Office to Profession: The New England Ministry, 1750–1850* (Philadelphia: University of Pennsylvania Press, 1978) and Ann Douglas, *The Feminization of American Culture* (New York: Alfred A. Knopf, 1977).

11 A forthcoming study by John Ohles cited in Tyack and Hansot, *Managers of Virtue,* p. 45. The influential role of the clergy in Needham is also detailed in Sylvia Olfson Shapiro, "Sources of Equality: Social Theory, Social History and Educational Policy," unpub. Ph.D. diss. (Harvard University, 1981). Furthermore, even though Alexander Field emphasizes the role of manufacturers in advocating educational reforms, the clergymen made up the largest single group of individuals on the Lowell School Board. See Alexander James Field, "Educational Reform and Manufacturing Development in Mid-Nineteenth Century Massachusetts," unpub. Ph.D. diss. (University of California, Berkeley, 1974), p. 54.

12 On the changing nature of the nineteenth-century ministry, see Scott, *From Office to Profession* and Daniel H. Calhoun, *Professional Lives in America: Structure and Aspiration, 1750–1850* (Cambridge: Harvard University Press, 1965).

13 Beverly *Citizen,* March 24, 1860.

14 For a very useful study of the relationship between an individual's religion and his partisan positions in the nineteenth century, see Melvyn Hammarberg, *The Indiana Voter: The Historical Dynamics of Party Allegiance During the 1870s* (Chicago: University of Chicago Press, 1977).

15 While there are many studies of party identification and voting behavior for the nineteenth century, there is much less work on the nature of office holding. For an introduction to some of these issues, see Edward Pessen, *Riches, Class, and Power before the Civil War* (Lexington, Mass.: D. C. Heath, 1973).

16 Although Katz does not specifically mention Frederick Choate, Choate played a leading role in the attempt to establish a public high school in Beverly (Katz, *Irony of Early School Reform,* pp. 23–27).

17 For a more satisfactory portrayal of Rantoul, see Arthur J. Newman, "Robert Rantoul: The Man and His Era," unpub. M.A. thesis (University of Maine, Orono, 1966).

18 Katz, *Irony of Early School Reform.*

19 Kaestle, *Pillars of the Republic.*

20 Ibid.

21 Not all workers were opposed to high schools. In fact, an editorial in the short-lived but important worker paper, the *Awl,* on March 8, 1845, called for the establishment of a public high school in Lynn. Therefore, scholars who say that antebellum workers were always against public high schools need to reconsider such strong statements. For a discussion of workers and education in Lynn, see Kaestle and Vinovskis, *Education and Social Change,* pp. 139–85.

22 Katz, *Irony of Early School Reform.*

23 Interestingly, the sympathetic Beverly *Citizen* suggested that the shoemakers should form a national and state alliance in order to achieve their goals since by that time it was clear that many employers would not agree to a set of prices because of the competition from workers in other communities who were not participating in the strike. Beverly *Citizen,* March 17, 1860.

24 Alexander James Field, "Economic and Demographic Determinants of Educational Commitment: Massachusetts, 1855," *Journal of Economic History* 39, no. 2 (June 1979): 439–59; Kaestle and Vinovskis, *Education and Social Change.* We have tried, however, to overcome this problem with an in-depth investigation of two communities, Lynn and Boxford.

25 On education in Boxford and Lynn, see Kaestle and Vinovskis, *Education and Social Change,* pp. 139–85. For a discussion of the great differences in nineteenth-century educational opportunities between small towns and rural areas, see Patricia Albjerg Graham, *Community and Class in American Education, 1865–1918* (New York: John Wiley, 1974).

26 Similarly, Luther Short, editor of a local newspaper in Johnson County, Indiana, initially vigorously opposed public high schools as too expensive and unnecessary in the 1870s, but by the 1890s he became reconciled or resigned to their existence and value. See Graham, *Community and Class in American Education,* pp. 27–67.

27 On the transformation of the antebellum shoe industry, see Alan Dawley, *Class and Community: The Industrial Revolution in Lynn* (Cambridge: Harvard University Press, 1976); Paul G. Faler, *Mechanics and Manufacturers in the Early Industrial Revolution, Lynn, Massachusetts, 1780–1860* (Albany, N.Y.: State University of New York Press, 1981).

28 On the trends in expenditures on the state level, see Kaestle and Vinovskis, *Education and Social Change,* pp. 186–207.

29 On the issue of education as human capital, see Maris A. Vinovskis, "Horace Mann on the Economic Productivity of Education," *New England Quarterly* 43, no. 4 (December 1970): 550–71.

Index

Abbot, Abiel (minister), 148n
Abbot, Abiel (schoolmaster), 62
Abbott, A. A., 79
Abbott, Joseph Hale, 106
academies, 61–65, 80, 94, 150n, 151n.
  See also Beverly Academy
age: and school attendance, 18–19; and
  vote on Beverly High School, 86–88
American Party, 153n
Andrews, Frank M., 156n
Angus, David L., 140n
Axtell, James, 150n

Baker, John I., 75, 84
Baker, John R., 81
Bernard, Richard M., 141n, 144n, 147n
Best, John Hardin, 140n
Beverly Academy, 32, 62–64, 69, 151n
Beverly *Citizen,* 70, 82–84, 91, 99–100,
  102, 106
Beverly Overseers of Poor, 50, 71
Beverly Public High School, 48, 56:
  abolition of, 5, 27, 59, 72, 83–108, 111;
  characteristics of supporters and opponents, 84–105, 107, 118, 138n, 139n,
  151n, 161n; enrollment in, 77–78, 80–
  83, 106; entrance requirements, 79–81,
  154n; establishment of, 5, 49, 56, 59,
  72, 79, 111, 152n; and grammer school,
  62; indictment against town, 5, 59, 75,
  77, 79, 81, 96, 103–7, 111; per pupil expenditure, 82; previous efforts to
  establish, 5, 56, 58, 59, 65–66, 68–73,
  109, 111; reestablishment of, 59, 105–6,
  108, 112, 115; site of, 69, 77–79, 81–84,
  105, 111, 162n; and workers, 7, 86–88,
  96–102, 107, 109, 158n
Beverly Town Meeting, 49; abolition of
  high school, 83–84; Citizen's Ticket,
  102–3; distribution of school funds, 55;
  establishment of high school, 56, 58,
  75; hiring of teachers, 55, 57–58, 83;
  previous efforts to establish high
  school, 58, 65, 70–71, 73; reestablishment of high school, 105–6, 108; selec-
  tion of site for high school, 77–79,
  81–84; shoe strike, 99; superintendent
  of schools, 68; turnout, 84–85, 156n
Bible, 149n
Bill of Wages, 159n
Binder, Frederick M., 151n
Boocock, Sarane Spence, 142n
Boston, Massachusetts, 44, 152n
Bowles, Samuel, 3, 10, 15, 24, 25, 27,
  138n, 140n, 141n, 144n, 145n
Boxford, Massachusetts, 20, 40, 44
Boyden, Albert, 154n
Boyden, James W., 151n
Boyden, Wyatt C., 51, 54, 59, 101
Boyer, Paul, 141n

DESIGNED BY BARBARA WERDEN
COMPOSED BY THE COMPOSING ROOM, INC., APPLETON, WISCONSIN
MANUFACTURED BY INTER-COLLEGIATE PRESS, INC.
SHAWNEE MISSION, KANSAS
TEXT AND DISPLAY LINES ARE SET IN TIMES ROMAN

Library of Congress Cataloging-in-Publication Data
Vinovskis, Maris.
The origins of public high schools.
Includes index.
1. High schools—Massachusetts—Beverly—History—
19th century. 2. Public schools—Massachusetts—
Beverly—History—19th century. 3. Beverly High School
—History—19th century. I. Title.
LA306.B48V56   1985   373.744′5   85-40380
ISBN 0-299-10400-1